Logos: Making a Strong Mark

ROCKPORT

CREATIVE ! SOLUTIONS

ROCKPORT PUBLISHERS

Logos: Making a Strong Mark

150 Strategies for Logos That Last

Anistatia Miller and Jared Brown

First published in the United States of America by
Rockport Publishers, Inc.
33 Commercial Street
Gloucester, Massachusetts 01930-5089
Telephone: (978) 282-9590
Fax: (978) 283-2742
www.rockpub.com

Library of Congress Cataloging-in-Publication Data

Miller, Anistatia R, [date]
    Logos : making a strong mark / Anistatia Miller & Jared Brown.
        p.   cm.
    Includes index.
    ISBN 1-59253-078-8 (hardcover)
    1. Logos (Symbols)—Design. I. Brown, Jared M., [date] II. Title.
NC1002.L63M54 2004
    741.6—dc222   004008679
                                                   CIP

ISBN 1-59253-078-8

10 9 8 7 6 5 4 3 2 1

Cover Design: Art & Anthropology
Spread Design: Collaborated, Inc.
Copy Editor: Madeline Perri
Proofreader: Ron Hampton

Printed in China

Dedication

Design succeeds through the passion and vision of both the designer and the client. For this reason, we dedicate this book to Stan Bratskeir and Rob Bratskeir— the most supportive "clients" and collaborators one could ever hope to find.

Contents

Introduction: **Memo from the Design
and Marketing Department**

Ever ask yourself why sales is associated with marketing, while design is connected to production? Certainly it makes sense for the designer to oversee production, if only to ensure the printer's or packager's execution matches the designer's vision. And the designer must have an intimate understanding of the limitations of production, which are also the limits of applied design. But this is only the vocational aspect of the designer's art and craft.

When it comes to creating strong logos, design and implementation are the last steps along a long path. The design of a visual identity is essential to the marketing of any brand because logos are marketing tools. And the only way to create a great logo—aside from blind luck—is to approach it first from the marketer's standpoint.

A marketing assessment is so logical and essential that most designers intuitively begin each project by analyzing their subject through marketing's six P's: product, place, price, packaging, promotion, and people. This assessment can be as informal as a moment's thought or the charting of the six P's on a notepad with the details sketched around them. Or the evaluation can take place over the course of months through research, interviews, focus groups, competitive analysis, test markets, and surveys.

Of course, any process can seem straightforward when it's viewed out of context. The logo designer's real challenge is to execute this feat of visual marketing prestidigitation while running a gauntlet of client demands, time constraints, saturated or shifting markets, divergent audiences, new technologies, and unusual applications.

The logos in this book are strong because they made it through these challenges—and many more—to reach their targets with maximum marketing impact and often impressive, measurable results. The designs run the gamut from elegant to industrial, frilly to macho, serious to silly, refined to unpolished, quirky to mainstream, striking to stark. Yet they have a common trait that sets them above the rest: They make a strong mark.

Clean shapes and simple lines assured Franke + Fiorella and JazzMn that this logo would be readable, both on stage and in print.

Client: **JazzMn**
Minneapolis, Minnesota, USA

Agency: **Franke + Fiorella**
Minneapolis, Minnesota

The Challenge

Founded in 1998, the nonprofit JazzMn's mission is to "promote, preserve, and perpetuate jazz through performance, the preservation of historical documents and artifacts, and through education." The organization's most visible component is JazzMn Big Band, a professional orchestra that combines the talents of musicians who hail from Minneapolis and St. Paul. Performances are an integral part of the organization's mission and a major source of its support. When JazzMn needed an identity that would appeal to audiences of all ages and be legible on drum sets and bandstands as well as on letterhead, it called on Minneapolis-based Franke + Fiorella.

The Process

The design firm followed a proven method for developing the identity. Beginning with a competitive audit and design exploration, they developed and refined numerous treatments. This led to a graphic treatment incorporating a highly stylized illustration of a brass instrument surrounded by a sleek type treatment, all within an oval. Keeping the shapes and lines clean and simple assured both the designers and the client that the image would be readable both on stage and in print.

The Result

Completing JazzMn's classic big band image, the brand identity not only appears—and is easy to recognize from a distance—on stage equipment and instruments, but it also looks equally appropriate on the organization's stationery, advertising campaigns, website, newsletters, programs, and tickets.

ZEPHYR

*The word zephyr—
the name of the Greek god
of the west wind—refers in
modern nautical terms to a
warm breeze. The smooth-
moving Z executed with
multicolored signal flag
stripes distills Greek mythology and maritime themes
into a cohesive whole.*

Client: **Circle Line Harbor Cruises LLC/Zephyr**
New York, New York, USA

Agency: **Lippincott Mercer**
New York, New York

The Challenge

A preeminent New York attraction for five decades, the Circle Line is an established source, offering full and half cruises around Manhattan Island as well as
cruises to the Statue of Liberty, seaport music cruises, harbor lights evening
cruises, Bear Mountain fall foliage cruises, and The Beast high-speed adventure
tours. In an effort to appeal to both upscale local and international target audiences as well as to commemorate 50 years of service, Circle Line called on
Lippincott Mercer to develop a brand for its newest offering—the *Zephyr*, a lavish
600-passenger high-speed catamaran, created by Austal USA, which offers a
smooth cruise around the New York waterways. The premium line is a unique
venue for catered parties from weddings and bar mitzvahs to corporate events.

The Process

To start, the Lippincott Mercer brand essence team collaborated with the client
in the naming process, selecting and screening names for Internet uniqueness,
intellectual-property rights clearance, and potential linguistic and cultural con-
flicts. The final candidate was the word *zephyr*, the name of the Greek god of the
west wind and, in modern nautical terms, a warm breeze. The team then developed a focused brand positioning statement, story, and supporting messages
around the company's mission and services roster.

Firmly basing their work on the company's positioning statement and mission,
the Lippincott Mercer design team developed type treatments, symbols, and
wordmarks, exploring Greek mythology and nautical themes including maritime
signal flags. The final solution expresses a nautical character woven into the
smooth-moving *Z* executed with multicolored signal flag stripes.

The Result

The Zephyr logo was applied to the catamaran itself, as well as to all the company's collateral, and was animated on its website, www.zephyrcruises.com. A
launch party, catered by the Circle Line's catering company, was held to christen
Zephyr's first harbor cruise on September 4, 2003.

*The concept of nautical
tone has changed radically
and now bears little to no
resemblance to traditional
nautical design. Rather, it
reflects the leisure and luxury of cruising.*

*The Zephyr, a lavish 600-
passenger high-speed
catamaran, offers a smooth
ride and upscale service
along the New York
waterways. It is based in
Manhattan's Hudson
River Park.*

INTREPID
SEA, AIR & SPACE MUSEUM   Adventures in Heroism

98pt6's redesigned logo communicates the name and physical structure more than the ship itself, while emphasizing the Intrepid's core message—heroism.

Client: **The Intrepid Sea, Air, and Space Museum**
New York, New York, USA

Agency: **98pt6**
New York, New York

The Challenge

Located on the Hudson River in midtown Manhattan, the Intrepid Sea, Air, and Space Museum has long appealed to a loyal core audience of war veterans and military buffs. But a general lack of awareness and cultural relevance caused recent visitor numbers to stagnate. The museum's existing visual brand was too masculine to appeal to a broad audience. Bottom line: To increase traffic and recognition, the museum had to update its brand image while remaining true to its military and historic equity.

The Process

The 98pt6 team was charged with identifying a new untapped target audience and creating an image that would resonate with the new target. After filtering through existing research and conducting interviews that disclosed current barriers and potential attractions to the brand, they pinpointed baby boomers with preteen children. They discovered that although Vietnam-era boomers reject a strong military brand of aggressiveness and war, they are strongly attracted to underlying military values—morals, character, and leadership.

Plays on the new logo's military ribbon motif bring the same strength of color and message to transit ads.

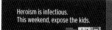

Body of steel.
Heart of gold.

The Result

Heroism became the brand's rallying cry, and leadership became its vision. New messaging—including the use of the tagline "Adventures in Heroism" in the final visual treatment—focused attention on the real lives of real heroes and the historic aircraft carrier that survived kamikaze attacks and served as the rescue vessel for the *Mercury* and *Gemini* NASA space missions. With military ribbons of honor as the overall design theme, a warm palette was fashioned into color bands that echo, but do not duplicate, actual military decorations. This simple device threads through the museum's signage, advertising, and collateral materials, reminding viewers that heroism can be found everywhere.

Condensed to colored borders, the logo motif effectively draws the attention of children, who were previously an underserved market for the Intrepid.

The new logo not only spawned a new line of branded merchandise but also birthed a new youth program on the Intrepid, in which children can "earn their stripes" by visiting exhibits and participating in activities.

Client: **ACT Theatre**
Seattle, Washington, USA

Agency: **Modern Dog Design Company**
Seattle, Washington

The Challenge

Creative clients can be demanding on a number of levels. When your client is a musician or an actor, you must remain objective as a designer, able to translate the client's personal tastes and wishes while instilling your own sense of form and logic into the equation. Modern Dog Design Company added a lot of patience to this to create the identity for the Seattle-based ACT Theatre, which produces contemporary work primarily by new playwrights. The theater's artistic director had spent six months with another design studio, trying to develop a mark that reflected his vision, before he called in Modern Dog.

The Process

Professionalism and a complete understanding of what the artistic director wanted led to numerous presentations to a variety of committees that oversee ACT Theatre's operations. A direct, dynamic typographic treatment was selected in the process, which Modern Dog applied to signage and mock tickets for a final, confirming presentation. Although the image is compact and wide, it works effectively in the vertical outdoor signage system that was purchased and installed before the logo design was finalized.

The Result

ACT Theatre, which was Seattle's first theater dedicated to new plays, loves the new identity. The Modern Dog design team feels that the identity's greatest success is the applause it received from the client, who called it a real step up from its previous small-town theater image.

The theater's artistic director spent six months with another studio before working with Modern Dog to create a contemporary image that reflected the company's repertoire without bias toward either drama or comedy.

Although the image is compact and wide, it works effectively in a stacked version on the vertical outdoor signage system that was purchased and installed before the logo design was finalized.

ACT Theatre's identity achieved its greatest success in the applause it received from the client, who feels it's a real step up from its previous small-town theater image.

The Sasquatch! logo draws on a long rock music legacy of psychedelic bands like the Grateful Dead, Jimi Hendrix, and Jefferson Airplane, yet it feels completely contemporary and speaks directly to the current diverse music-loving audience.

Client: **House of Blues**
            Bellevue, Washington, USA

Agency: **Modern Dog Design Company**
            Seattle, Washington

The Challenge

Sasquatch! is an annual music festival produced by House of Blues. Staged in The Gorge, a natural amphitheater carved out by the Columbia River near George, Washington, the show is a twelve-hour, three-stage indie-rock marathon. Modern Dog was approached to create a logotype that would stand on its own and accompany the existing Sasquatch! icon. No strangers to tight deadlines, Modern Dog dove in with a week to produce the final design.

The Process

With as much passion for indie rock as professional design, Modern Dog's designers pored over the list of bands playing at Sasquatch! Their familiarity with the bands' visuals and music industry design trends led them straight to their sketchpads, where half a dozen sketches produced a rough that quickly was approved and refined into its final form: a retro form that draws heavily from 1960s and 1970s imagery.

The Result

The Sasquatch! logo achieves its purpose: It draws on a long rock music legacy, yet feels contemporary and speaks directly to the current diverse music-loving audience. Under the new Sasquatch! mark, acts ranging from Coldplay to Galactic to String Cheese Incident performed for more than 20,000 concertgoers.

This shirt design for the Sasquatch! Music Festival draws heavily from 1960s and 1970s imagery made famous by posters designed by Family for the Fillmore West and other venues.

Modern Dog created a younger, hipper cousin of the Washington State Lottery's Lotto image; it needed to stand on its own as well as coexist with the previous logo during a three-year transition.

Client: **Publicis**
Seattle, Washington, USA

Agency: **Modern Dog Design Company**
Seattle, Washington

The Challenge

Ultimately, it's not what the designer wants but what the client needs that drives logo design. When a brand is recognized by millions of people, improvements must be subtle. In the case of the Washington State Lottery's Lotto logo, this challenge was compounded by a plan for the gradual introduction of the new identity, creating a three-year overlap in which both the old and new logos would be in use. For Modern Dog, this redesign meant carefully selecting which elements would be preserved and which elements would be worked on to effect a hipper, more exciting brand without confusing the brand's huge existing customer base.

The Process

The Modern Dog team studied the current logo and all its applications. Although they reworked the type, they incorporated similar colors in the updated version to minimize confusion.

The Result

The new Lotto logo is now being phased in by Publicis, Washington State Lottery's advertising agency, on everything from TV commercials to outdoor signage to lottery tickets. As one member of the Modern Dog team said, "Our client is so thrilled, it makes the project a success story for us."

Elements of playfulness and the indisputable thrill of a chance win suffuse Lotto's print materials.

A simplified version of Modern Dog's new logo appears on all lottery tickets.

RealActionPictures
Stock Footage

Real Action Pictures' logo portrays the wilder edge of waves, ski tracks, tire tracks, and mountains in three simple lines—the focus of the company's documentary action and extreme-sports stock footage.

The Real Action Pictures's website conveys everything the company does, from traveling the world to capturing footage of exotic landscapes.

Client: **Real Action Pictures**
Calgary, Alberta, Canada

Agency: **Morpheus Studios, Inc.**
Calgary, Alberta

The Challenge
Real Action Pictures shoots and produces three adventure television series as well as documentary action stock footage. The production company has an extensive catalog of surfing, snowboarding, and other extreme-sports footage as well as clips of tropical sunsets, waves, and other natural features shot in exotic locations around the world.

Real Action Pictures' cutting-edge, hip TV and movie programming needed to be visually represented with a brandmark that wouldn't become outdated in a few years. The real challenge faced by the design studio, Morpheus, was that the company's brand image needed to be simple yet symbolize so many things: action, waves, nature, and a fresh style of film production. The identity also had to be usable in a variety of formats and be cost-effective to reproduce.

The Process
Morpheus's founder, Greg MacDonald, started his exploration by viewing some of the company's footage and realizing what drives Real Action Pictures to do what they do. He quickly discovered everything the company does relates to traveling the world and capturing footage of exotic landscapes and the men and women who try to tame, conquer, or just get an adrenaline buzz from these locations—in short, humans in nature and nature in motion.

After playing with several geometric concepts that expressed film and motion, the Morpheus team focused on developing a few ideas around a loose strip of film that could be shaped into a wave, a mountain, or a sand dune. The team then overlapped the images to catch the many forms captured by Real Action Pictures' cameras.

The Result
In addition to appearing on their equipment at shoots in exotic and wild locations around the world, the brand identity was the starting point for a complete rebranding of the Real Action Pictures' group of companies. The finished logo was an integral part of the company's new website design.

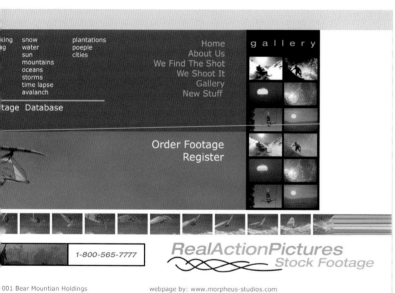

Morpheus Studios' logo for RAP International—Real Action's group of companies—reflects nature and a fresh style of film production. This sub-brand treatment provides the necessary cohesiveness the company needed to convey its message to its clients.

The Chicago-based theater group Running with Scissors prides itself on breaking the rules and creating original material. Its name plays on the adage "Don't run with scissors!" But as many people know, great things can happen when you break the rules and take chances.

The Running with Scissors logo pays homage to the child found in everyone and is applied to T-shirts worn by the production company and loyal patrons.

Client: **Running with Scissors**
Chicago, Illinois, USA

Agency: **Richard Zeid Design**
Evanston, Illinois

The Challenge

The Chicago-based theater group Running with Scissors was founded in 1999 by fourteen performance artists of diverse backgrounds. The group is committed to creating art that is rigorously inventive, timely, and provocative, seeking to examine the social, political, and cultural landscapes of our times. The theater company prides itself on breaking the rules and creating original material in a theater-rich city. The challenge faced by Richard Zeid Design was to create a logo with no concrete context, reflecting the theater's openness.

The Process

Through extensive dialogue with the Running with Scissors creative team, the Richard Zeid Design team unearthed the energy the troupe brings to their productions. As Richard Zeid commented, "They were very much like kids playing and creating work from their imaginations and not worrying about the 'adults' out there saying 'You can't do that!'" Many people have heard the adage "Don't run with scissors!" But as many people know, great things can happen when you bend and break the rules.

The Result

The Richard Zeid Design team's solution pays homage to the raucous, rambunctious child in everyone. The result is a warm, easily recognizable brand image that beckons viewers to enter a world of limitless discovery. The name has also produced subbrands such as SNIPS (Scissors New Work in Progress).

Applied with other elements on promotional posters, the Running with Scissors logo retains its strength, even when used in a small size.

Client: **The *Fader* Magazine**
New York, New York, USA

Agency: **Staple Design**
New York, New York, and Tokyo, Japan

Catering to a Gen-Y audience, the international music magazine Fader presents the edgy side of pop culture. Staple Design's logo for the publication is reminiscent of punk-era British publications like The Face.

The Challenge

Catering to a Gen-Y audience, the international music magazine *Fader* presents pop culture ranging from new music and cutting-edge fashion to inspired photography and innovative film in a unique "new journalism" style. Amid a sea of similar publications targeting the same market, the bimonthly magazine needed an identity that would jump ahead of its competitors on the newsstands without battling other cover elements. The logo also had to resonate with its young, demanding readership. To accomplish this not-so-simple task, the publishers called on Staple Design.

The Process

As Staple Design's Jeffrey C. Ng admitted, the process of creating a visual identity that could hold up in a variety of colors accompanied by an even greater number of illustrative elements took "dozens and dozens of revisions." Each concept had to be tested against potential cover photos of the White Stripes, Yeah Yeah Yeahs, and Outkast, plus additional typography. The final result was a raw, sans-serif type treatment reminiscent of punk-era British publications like *The Face*.

The Result

The beauty of *Fader's* finished logo lies in its sparse, clean design, which will allow it to function without appearing dated as each season's styles and tastes give way to those of the next. In the music industry, styles change rapidly and freshness is essential.

Fader's logo works well in a variety of colors, set against strong, award-winning photography. It also works in an iconic version on the bimonthly publication's website (not shown here).

Client: **Zamboni**
Paramount, California, USA

Agency: **Walk Design**
Rocky Hill, Connecticut, USA

The Challenge

Everyone who has ever been to an ice skating rink or seen a professional hockey game has watched with awe as the Zamboni cleaned the ice between periods. The manufacturer of the ice resurfacer, the California-based Zamboni Company, decided it was time to refresh its identity for use on a line of promotional items: headgear, hockey wear, T-shirts, collectibles, accessories, novelties, and remote-control replicas. The company asked a number of designers to submit proposals.

The Process

"I really was pretty green when it came to working with a client and understanding that it wasn't necessarily what I wanted but what the client wanted with my creative thought process mixed in," Matthew Walker of Walk Design admitted. But he felt fortunate in one respect: He'd grown up watching the Zambonis clear the ice at New York Rangers games and had always been fascinated by them, making his design job a lot simpler.

Walker faced two major challenges in this project. It was his first professional identity job, and he had well-seasoned competition. Walker decided to make his submission a fun visual that could be seen even from the worst seats in Madison Square Garden. Reminiscent of superhero emblems, the Zamboni *Z* is the focal point of the oval-framed logo. Walker selected a bright blue and black color palette that would also appeal to younger audiences. The client chose his solution.

Zamboni's three-dimensional logo speaks of the ice resurfacer's superhero persona as it glides along the ice skating rink. In a two-dimensional version, it serves as an emblem used on promotional items and the company's website.

The Zamboni Z is used as an icon, reflecting the ice resurfacer's motion on the skating rink. Here, it's employed as an insignia on a sports cap.

The Result

Walker's logo has been used in a variety of ways since its unveiling. Although it was originally employed on promotional items, the company eventually used the design on the ice resurfacing machines themselves. Now, new generations of kids have a recognizable symbol to remember as they watch the Zambonis clear the ice.

The full Zamboni logo has been applied on a line of promotional items: head-gear, hockey wear, T-shirts, collectibles, accessories, novelties, and remote-control replicas.

Client: **Mill Valley Film Festival**
Mill Valley, California, USA

Agency: **FutureBrand**
New York, New York, USA

The Mill Valley Film Festival logo makes effective use of light and shadow, reflecting the flexibility of film and the mountainous landscape of the event's location.

The Mill Valley Film Festival's Marin County location has helped make it one of California's longest-running, best-attended film industry events. Because the festival presents numerous film genres, its logo needed to reflect the event's location more than its content.

The Challenge

Film festivals offer both presenters and viewers an opportunity to concentrate on a specific genre: foreign, independent, animation—the list goes on and on. In more than 25 years, the Mill Valley Film Festival has earned its global reputation as a high-profile celebration of international cinema. It is America's fourth-largest film event and California's longest-running fall festival. Committed to launching both American and foreign independent projects, the 11-day festival stages features, documentaries, shorts, new media, and video, hosting about 200 international filmmakers. The festival presents more than conventional celluloid motion pictures; it also exhibits original video and digital works. To commemorate its 25th anniversary, festival organizers called on FutureBrand to refresh its brand image. The new visual brand had to encompass the Festival's multimedia point of difference and its emotional legacy. It also had to be relevant to the film industry's future.

The Process

The FutureBrand team conducted extensive interviews with participants and festivalgoers as well as an audit of the hundreds of film festivals held around the world. The team presented a range of concepts from simple typography to a symbol of postproduction technology. Four finalists were selected, each with its own champion among the Festival board of film industry leaders. The winner not only reflected the festival's broad media scope but also scenic landmarks of its Marin County location—Muir Woods and Mount Tamalpais.

The Result

The final visual image was initially applied to letterhead, business cards, invitations, and programs. It was then employed in both cinema and local public broadcasting system station commercials for a month prior to the festival. The 2002 launch of the Mill Valley Film Festival's new identity signaled a change in the way the festival was marketed. In fact, the 2002–2003 season was its most successful ever.

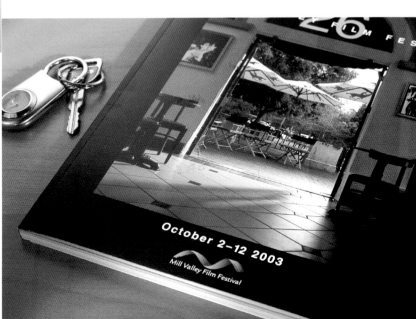

VOOM is an exciting new home entertainment service that offers more than 30 true HDTV-quality programming channels with heightened visuals, sound quality, and cinema-style screen format. FutureBrand's logo and name reflect the impact the service has on its viewers.

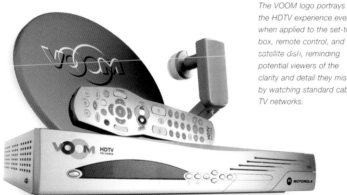

The VOOM logo portrays the HDTV experience even when applied to the set-top box, remote control, and satellite dish, reminding potential viewers of the clarity and detail they miss by watching standard cable TV networks.

Client: **VOOM**
Bethpage, New York, USA

Agency: **FutureBrand**
New York, New York

The Challenge

High-definition television (HDTV) offers viewers heightened visuals, enhanced sound quality, and cinema-style screen format. With the development of HDTV monitors and broadcast equipment came the launch of a revolutionary new cable network carrying more than thirty HDTV-quality programming channels that offer movies, sports, music, and more every day. FutureBrand was commissioned to create a brand to announce this exciting new home entertainment service.

The Process

FutureBrand studied consumer research to understand precisely why people might want multichannel, commercial-free HDTV programming and what their expectations of this service were. The creative team generated hundreds of names and visuals, each expressing a different aspect of the cable network's business. The one candidate that offered the desired impact was the word VOOM.

Most station names are acronyms of the parent company's name, such as American Broadcasting Company (ABC), National Broadcasting Company (NBC), and Home Box Office (HBO). Other names spell out the station's content, such as the History Channel, Discovery Channel, and the Food Network. The toughest job FutureBrand faced was convincing the client that having a name that eschewed these conventions was the right brand strategy. Consumer testing validated the team's belief: People couldn't get the name out of their minds. VOOM was a winner!

The team portrayed the HDTV experience in every aspect of the logo. Primary and secondary screen pixel colors make up the identity's color palette. All printed literature is constructed according to HDTV's 9:16 screen proportions and employs oversized and crisply detailed imagery—reminding potential viewers of the clarity and detail they miss by watching standard cable TV networks.

The Result

On the station's launch day in 2003, the logo appeared in 6-inch-high letters on a full-page advertisement in the *New York Times*. VOOM's brand power is already evident; the press has embraced the brand in headlines such as "Room to VOOM," indicating that it's well on its way to becoming part of the cultural vernacular. As one new customer said in an exit interview, "I can hardly wait to go and tell my friends I've got VOOM."

Since its launch, the VOOM brand had been embraced by the press in headlines such as "Room to VOOM," indicating that it's well on its way to becoming part of the cultural vernacular. The logo, applied on service trucks, imprints the company's strong message on the street.

Client: **London Tourist Board/Visit London**
London, UK

Agency: **Wolff Olins**
London, UK

The Challenge

London has so many locally based businesses and institutions that use the word London in their names the city's uniqueness is often taken for granted by residents and visitors. In fact, the word *London* had become trite. The London Tourist Board approached Wolff Olins to create a new brand identity, commissioning the agency to develop a name and a logo that reflected the structural changes in London tourism. Besides needing a modern and dynamic municipal brand, the board also had to more closely ally its identity with other British tourism organizations such as Visit Britain and Visit Scotland.

The Process

The Wolff Olins team concentrated its research efforts on two target audiences, surveying visitors and residents on their perceptions of the city. Both discordant and surprising, the solution changed the way people see the word *London*. Broken into two stacked syllables, the image offers viewers two portals through which they can view the city. The versatile basic image allows London's diversity and wealth of attractions and achievements to be presented in a template that is instantly recognizable and highly legible. Contrast plays a major role in the image's implementation: Big Ben pairs off with British Airways' London Eye; St. Paul's Cathedral is juxtaposed with the Gherkin; the Phantom of the Opera's mask contrasts with Shakespeare's Globe Theatre.

The Result

The new logo is used in a vast range of merchandise and promotional materials, including the official website, www.visitlondon.com, which provides visitors with travel, planning, and current events information. The new brand has helped increase interest in numerous London attractions of which visitors were previously unaware.

Wolff Olins' solution for Visit London is versatile enough to portray the many attractions that draw visitors to this diverse city. The Phantom of the Opera's mask contrasts with Shakespeare's Globe Theatre [above]. Big Ben pairs off with British Airways' 140-meter-tall London Eye [right]. And London's Underground Tube logo is juxtaposed with the classic London black cab [far right].

Sha Boom Boom himself loves the identity so much he brands it with a rubber stamp on members of the audience at each show. The logo is also used on all promotional posters for the performances.

Americans with Disabilities Act (ADA) symbols were combined with a strong type treatment to portray gender transformations. The arrows and stars impress the entertainment quality and level of surprise found in Sha Boom Boom's performance.

Gender Illusionist Technician Sha Boom Boom's business card communicates the costume and gender transformations he makes in his performances.

Client: **Sha Boom Boom**
Brooklyn, New York, USA

Agency: **The Missive**
New York, New York, USA

The Challenge
Keith Venter is a performance artist who labels himself a "gender illusionist technician" and whose stage name is Sha Boom Boom. He wanted a polished, clean identity that also communicates the costume and gender transformations he makes in his performances.

As The Missive's Julian Leon admitted, "I never imagined creating a logo for a drag queen. This type of performance art is difficult to associate with images beyond the wigs and makeup that are superficial to the art form."

The Process
Leon witnessed Sha Boom Boom's on-stage transformation and tried to capture the work behind Venter's illusion. Then he embarked on creating a visual explanation, focusing on the entertainment aspect and its delightful twist. A Futura Xtra Bold type treatment was selected to emphasize the onomatopoetic quality of Venter's stage name. Americans with Disabilities Act (ADA) symbols were combined to portray gender differences. The two shapes share a head, communicating to viewers the polarity of the individual. The arrows and stars impress the entertainment and transformational qualities of Sha Boom Boom's performance.

The Result
The Missive's bold solution was a total hit. Sha Boom Boom himself loves the identity so much he brands it with a rubber stamp onto members of the audience at each show.

The use of ligatures and painted letterforms in Dancing Life's logo increases the fluidity and humanity of the name and implies merging energies.

Dancing Life's website avoids the use of New Age symbols for yoga, shiatsu, and reiki, instead stressing the company's mission to provide its patrons with the tools for self-empowerment through use of body energy.

Client:
Dancing Life—Body Energy for Self-Empowerment
Forest Hills, New York, USA

Agency:
The Missive
New York, New York

The Challenge

Subjects with a New Age or healthy living message often fall into the same visual traps as corporate identities. Visual clichés may be a comfortable place for a designer to explore, but they do little to create a marketable point of difference for the client. Dancing Life's mission is to provide its patrons with the tools for self-empowerment through use of body energy. It also offers sessions in yoga, shiatsu, and reiki. The Missive was asked to create an identity that portrayed the nurturing, flowing, and merging nature of human energy.

The Process

Every design exploration needs a direction. In The Missive's case, all roads led to a goal that did not include pictographs or symbols related to yoga, shiatsu, or reiki in the presentation. Going to Dancing Life's studio and gaining first-hand experience in a shiatsu session provided further inspiration. This led to experiments in the use of ligatures in the typographic treatment to convey merging energies and then to painted letterforms to increase the fluidity and humanity of the letterforms. Insignia was chosen as the secondary typeface for its geometric rigidity and Asian characteristics.

The Result

Yin and yang (warm and cool) energies are signified by the soft blue and yellow color palette that completes Dancing Life's meditative visual identity. The Missive's extra effort—taking time to experience the client's classes—is readily apparent in the final mark, which also uses thoughtful type treatments to convey the tone and personality of the client.

Sometimes you may prefer...

All of these approaches focus on energy awareness and honor you as an evolving creative person. It will help to increase your energy awareness and to develop a connection with yourself for a greater balance of mind, body and spirit.

Shiatsu

Shiatsu is a system of health touch based on the Asian approach to healing. Instead of focusing on muscle groups as in western massage, Lisa will stimulate the meridians, or energy pathways in your body. The concept is to treat the whole individual, body, mind and spirit.

You will lie on the floor on a comfortable surface and receive supportive pressure, exercise and stretching for a profound energy-sensing experience. Common sensations you might feel are tingling and a strong impulse that spreads

Yin and yang (warm and cool) energies are signified by the soft blue and yellow color palette used in Dancing Life's stationery program.

Manhattan Films

The client came with the basis for this logo—the icon. The Missive subtly bowed to tradition, adding the sprocket holes of a filmstrip to the identity for the film production company.

Client: **Manhattan Films**
New York, New York, USA

Agency: **The Missive**
New York, New York

The Challenge

Creative crutches are not limited to the realm of writers. Designers can also fall into the trap of utilizing cliché imagery to convey a thought. Filmmaking is a subject fraught with visual islands: filmstrips, clapboards, cameras, projectors, black backgrounds. This was the first challenge faced by The Missive in the design of Manhattan Films' identity. The second was the client's request to incorporate a visual created by the film company's president himself. Originally commissioned to design the company's website, The Missive team offered to update the logo in an effort to achieve overall visual cohesiveness.

The Process

To convey Manhattan Films' mission to acquire, develop, and produce a broad range of theater and television content, The Missive subtly bowed to the use of one traditional visual island in its Bodoni and proprietary dot-matrix font type treatment: the sprocket holes found on the edges of a filmstrip. But instead of attempting to parallel the concept of the ball element, they used a contrasting contextual approach to better effect. The Missive drew inspiration from surrealist Rene Magritte's paintings, floating the original logo like an all-seeing eye over a cityscape. This secondary icon is employed as a stand-alone on the company's letterhead and website.

The Result

Although Manhattan Films' website was the primary reason for and application of The Missive's logo design update, the logo has since been adapted for use on the company's stationery program and presentation materials. However, it is as background on the Web pages that the logo really comes to life in myriad variations, accompanied by a variety of complementary art.

Using Bodoni and a proprietary dot-matrix font type treatment, Manhattan Films' business cards expand on the filmstrip motif, framing both the icon and the typographic treatment in individual film frames.

Manhattan Films' website creates maximum impact with the icon by adding a cityscape, which draws its inspiration from surrealist Rene Magritte's paintings.

Manhattan Films

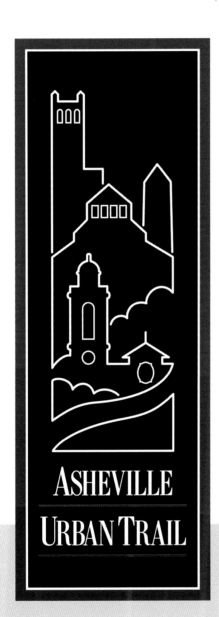

ASHEVILLE
URBAN TRAIL

Client: **Asheville Area Arts Council Urban Trail**
Asheville, North Carolina, USA

Agency: **Design One, Inc.**
Asheville, North Carolina

The Challenge

The Asheville Area Arts Council developed a walking tour to promote tourism in the city's downtown area as well as to acquaint residents with the area's rich history. Filled with architectural landmarks and other points of interest, the 30 station self-guided walking tour needed an identity that would identify stops along the way. The challenge Design One faced in the creation of this identity was the length of the name—Asheville Urban Trail—which had to be legible along the trail itself as well as on planned promotional items.

The Process

Initially, the design team suggested using footprints to represent the trail, but that proved too limiting and not in keeping with the character of the city when placed in context. Typographic solutions were also explored, but, once again, the concept didn't visually reflect either the city or the trail.

After numerous pencil sketches, four downtown Asheville architectural landmarks that are also stops on the trail were hand-drawn, scanned, and simplified. The drawings were stacked to capture the feel of the trail winding its way through the city's hilly streets. A condensed serif type treatment and a black and red color scheme added overall legibility to the mark.

The Result

The Asheville Urban Trail's new mark, which debuted in 2003, now adorns banners throughout downtown Asheville and appears on T-shirts and other popular merchandise the Arts Council sells at the Urban Trail Arts Festival and at the downtown visitors' center.

Asheville Area Arts Council Urban Trail's logo ascends the area's hilly streets through a staggered portrayal of its architectural gems. The design appears on signage along the self-guided tour, T-shirts, and other merchandise.

THE CENTER FOR CRAFT, CREATIVITY & DESIGN

The mission of the Center for Craft, Creativity, and Design is apparent in its encapsulated logo and classic typographic treatment.

Client: **Center for Craft, Creativity, and Design**
Hendersonville, North Carolina, USA

Agency: **Design One, Inc.**
Asheville, North Carolina

The Challenge

The Center for Craft, Creativity, and Design is an interinstitutional University of North Carolina public-service center whose mission is to support the advancement and integration of craft, creativity, and design. It carries out this work by promoting lifelong learning and providing solutions for the community through research, education, and community collaboration.

When Design One was contracted to design the organization's identity, it faced two major challenges: The center's name is very long, and its mission is multifaceted.

The Process

The design team explored numerous ways to express the center's core disciplines—craft, creativity, and design. A stylized typographic solution emerged as the most viable solution to the creation of an icon. The shapes of the letterforms CCCD drove the decision to encapsulate the letters that represent the disciplines inside the *C* of Center. A crisp, letterspaced treatment of the name balances underneath the icon—a graphic reminiscent of typographic works created by early twentieth-century master printers.

The Result

The arts and crafts style of the logo is a prefect marriage of the arts and crafts architecture to the center itself. The center's bold new icon and word mark have been implemented on the CCCD website and a stationery program and will be employed in future collateral and promotional projects.

CCCD's stationery system ensures that all correspondence perpetuates the organization's public service misssion.

THE CENTER
FOR CRAFT,
CREATIVITY
& DESIGN

POST OFFICE BOX 1127
HENDERSONVILLE, NC 28793

THE CENTER
FOR CRAFT,
CREATIVITY
& DESIGN

ph 828 890 2050 *fax* 828 890 2060
POST OFFICE BOX 1127 HENDERSONVILLE, NC 28793

THE CENTER
FOR CRAFT,
CREATIVITY
& DESIGN

JUDITH BARBER
FOUNDING DIRECTOR

ph 828 890 2050
fax 828 890 2060
judibarber@aol.com

POST OFFICE BOX 1127
HENDERSONVILLE, NC 28793

Minnesota
Public
Radio

A leader in publicly supported programming, Minnesota Public Radio expressed its growth and maturity as a broadcast content provider with a new logo design, which is paired with numerous radio call numbers on lockups.

Client: **Minnesota Public Radio**
St. Paul, Minnesota, USA

Agency: **Desgrippes Gobé Group**
New York, New York, USA

The Challenge

In the nationwide network of publicly supported television and radio stations, Minnesota Public Radio (MPR) is a leader in syndicated programming. The station produces shows such as the long-running *Prairie Home Companion* with Garrison Keillor, *American RadioWorks*, and *The Savvy Traveler.* It also broadcasts nationally syndicated radio shows such as *All Things Considered.*

To reflect its growth and maturity as a broadcast content provider, MPR called in Desgrippes Gobé Group to refresh its identity. Besides facing the challenge of visually communicating the concepts of radio and sound, the design team had to work with a lengthy name and the need for the identity to work in conjunction with various radio call numbers.

The Process

The Desgrippes Gobé team explored radio's visual territory as "a fertile refuge"— a private, emotional place in which a listener can learn and reflect. The team also explored the root of all meaningful communication and connection—people. Expanding ripples made by a raindrop as it gently touches the surface of placid water was the image that resonated through numerous sketches. The blue and gold color palette and clean typographic treatment add accessibility to the design.

**MINNESOTA
PUBLIC RADIO**

Though MPR's old black-and-white logo was functional, over time, refreshment seemed desirable.

Expanding ripples made by a raindrop as it gently touches the surface of placid water reflect the broadcaster's position as a calming refuge for listeners.

Brochure templates and banners that bear the new logo, color palette, and the tagline Radio That Matters herald the broadcaster's new position as a mature and growing syndicated content provider.

The Result

The finished identity is a distinctive and highly effective portrayal of impact. The client was extremely pleased and has applied it to a variety of materials ranging from stationery items and business cards to lockups with accompanying radio call numbers. Brochure templates and banners were also branded with the new MPR logo and color palette.

FRONT

JAM SHAKWI :: PRESIDENT
JAMSHAKWI@AOL.COM
(212) 967-1057 EXT 22

BACK

*Festive fonts were selected
to convey Wild Rainbow
Party's upbeat and varie-
gated personality and the
organization's promise to
create a party that draws
together people from all
sorts of backgrounds.*

*A recurrent symbol in gay
festive events—a rapidly
spinning rainbow flag—
serves as a focal point in
The Missive's solution for
this logo.*

Client:	**Wild Rainbow Party**
	New York, New York, USA
Agency:	**The Missive**
	New York, New York

The Challenge

Population groups fall victim to visual categorization, just as businesses and pro-
fessions do. Wild Rainbow Party produces documentary-style events such as the
White Party and Mardi Gras that target a gay audience. The organization also
creates and distributes documentary-style travel videos of these productions.
The Missive's challenge in taking on this identity project was to create a visual
that encompassed the organization's core market while steering clear of demographic profiles.

Though frequently identified in marketing and business plans as a lucrative market
with high disposable income, the gay population is, of course, extremely diverse.
This diversity makes it impossible to pigeonhole a specific image vocabulary that
will appeal to every target viewer. The Missive faced two additional visual handi-
caps in designing this identity: the client's name is fairly long, and the rainbow—
a universal symbol for the gay movement—had to be employed, creating a com-
plication when visual harmony had to be reached in the overall solution.

The Process

In the design exploration phase, The Missive searched for a way to establish
a relation among the words *wild rainbow party*. Festive fonts were selected to
convey the audience's upbeat and variegated personality and the organization's
promise to create a party that draws together people from all sorts of backgrounds. A recurrent symbol of gay festive events was used as an illustrative
element: the rapidly spinning rainbow flag.

The Result

The new festive, swirling brand has become a call to party for its broad target
audience. While the rainbow flag could be in danger of overbranding in the gay
community, this unique take on the established icon imbues it with freshness
and vitality.

*The Missive's challenge in
taking on this identity project was to create a visual
that encompassed the organization's core market, symbolized by the rainbow—a
universal symbol of the gay
movement. The image also
had to steer clear of demographic profiles.*

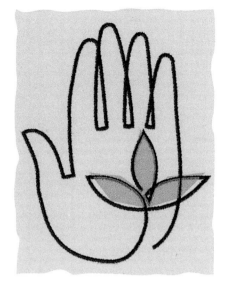

A continuous line drawing of a hand and a plant iconically represent the North Carolina Arboretum's tagline, "Cultivating a Living Treasure."

Cultivating A Living Treasure

Client: **North Carolina Arboretum**
Asheville, North Carolina, USA

Agency: **Design One, Inc**
Asheville, North Carolina

The Challenge

An affiliated, nonprofit facility of the 16 campus University of North Carolina system, the North Carolina Arboretum was established in the mid-1980s to serve the Blue Ridge communities of western North Carolina. A 426-acre public garden, seminars, and nature walks for both adults and children are just a few of the facility's offerings. According to its mission statement, the arboretum cultivates connections between people and plants through conservation, education, garden demonstration, economic development, and research.

To expand its facilities and programs, arboretum administrators launched a multimillion-dollar capital improvement campaign. The initiative called for the design of a mark that would be a visual call to action, one that would remind viewers of the bond between people and plants.

The Process

Design One was assigned the job of developing the mark, which had to carry the tagline "Cultivating a Living Treasure." The design team chose a continuous line drawing of a hand and a plant as the ideal representation of the organization's core message. The drawing was scanned, traced in Freehand software, and then imported into Photoshop, where it was roughened up to appear more raw and natural. A clear condensed type treatment and fresh green color scheme completed the identity's overall theme.

The Result

Like the plants it represents, the integration of this important new brand is taking on an organic form. The campaign's identity was first seen in the organization's stationery program and a 20-page campaign booklet that highlights the arboretum's accomplishments and the goals of the capital improvement campaign. Further uses will be considered as fund-raising continues.

Cultivating A
Living Treasure

A Campaign For
The North Carolina
Arboretum

Honorary Chairs

Molly Corbett Broad
President
University of North Carolina

John L. Creech
Former Director
United States National Arboretum

William C. Friday
President Emeritus
University of North Carolina

C. D. Spangler, Jr.
President Emeritus
University of North Carolina

Campaign Chair
Philip G. Carson

*The North Carolina Arboretum
Board of Directors*
William C. Seward
— Chair

*The North Carolina
Arboretum Society*
Todd N. Morse
President

The North Carolina Arboretum
George B. Briggs
Executive Director

The North Carolina Arboretum
100 Frederick Law Olmsted Way
Asheville, NC 28806-9315
Phone (828) 665-2492
Fax (828) 665-2371
www.ncarboretum.org

Cultivating A
Living Treasure

A Campaign For
The North Carolina
Arboretum

The North Carolina Arboretum
100 Frederick Law Olmsted Way
Asheville, NC 28806-9315

Cultivating A
Living Treasure

A Campaign For
The North Carolina
Arboretum

The Arboretum's use of natural fiber paper in its stationery system reinforces the facility's investment in conservation and nature education.

GEFFRYE MUSEUM
English Domestic Interiors

The Geffrye Museum's "through the keyhole" message invites visitors to explore the intimate room sets and discover hidden facets of British culture.

Client: **Geffrye Museum**
London, UK

Agency: **Lewis Moberly**
London, UK

The Challenge

The Geffrye Museum is a registered nonprofit organization based in London's East End, committed to preserving examples of British home interiors. The museum houses a permanent exhibition of interiors and gardens dating from 1600 to the present day and offering a compelling look into the metamorphosis of British interior design. The Geffrye called on Lewis Moberly to create a visual identity portraying the museum's distinctive nature and appeal while helping convey the institution's uniqueness in a city filled with museums and galleries dedicated to special-interest collections.

The Process

In auditing the elements necessary to create the perfect brand image, the Lewis Moberly design team became fascinated with the museum's showrooms: a series of eighteenth-century almshouses. Each small space leads to another, creating an Alice in Wonderland–like experience for visitors. Major exhibitions that change quarterly complement the permanent collection. The team focused on conveying a "through the keyhole" message of invitation to explore the intimate room sets and discover hidden facets of British culture.

The former logo presented the museum as alive and quaint, and yet kept viewers outside the fence.

The Result

Applied to museum signage, literature, posters, and website (www.geffrye-museum.org.uk), the Lewis Moberly visual brand has helped distinguish this off-the-beaten-path East End museum on Kingsland Road from London's many tourist attractions, making it a must-see destination.

The logo's keyhole concept was also translated into environmental graphics, such as the design of this entryway to one of the museum's almshouses.

Even a sterling silver spoon on a folded napkin emulates the museum's keyhole shape in this Lewis Moberly–designed poster.

Cutting Edge – An exhibition of English cutlery and place settings

Client: **JohnsonDiversey**
Sturtevant, Wisconsin, USA

Agency: **Lippincott Mercer**
New York New York, USA

The Challenge

A leader in the Lippincott Mercer design team was charged by JohnsonDiversey to create a brand image that communicated the union of two companies—Johnson Wax Professional and DiverseyLever—whose combined and complementary capabilities afford greater market share in the cleaning products, services, and management industry while retaining a brand equity link with both firms' existing customer bases in more than 60 countries. The challenge also required the team to engage in name development and brand positioning initiatives as well.

The Process

More than 1,300 names were selected and vetted through preliminary legal, linguistic, and Internet screenings before the best candidates were identified. The Lippincott Mercer team then conducted extensive executive and customer interviews plus an audit and review of numerous media and analyst reports before crafting a focused brand positioning statement. The design team then concurrently developed creative solutions—including logotypes, symbols, and wordmarks—for a visual review of all the candidates and the final selection process. The negation of space between the partners' names placed under a decorative icon that implies freshness, growth, and cleanliness highlights the fully executed solution.

The Result

When the final design solution was approved, the design team applied JohnsonDiversey's new identity to the marketing collateral system, presentation materials, corporate stationery, and signage. The team also designed a Day One launch brochure and microsite that enhanced the identity with the tagline "Clean is just the beginning." The team also crafted an online identity standards manual to effectively and efficiently manage the brand's further application.

JohnsonDiversey

Sometimes an identity is best defined by what's missing. White space is essential to communicating cleanliness in JohnsonDiversey's logo and collateral materials. Lippincott Mercer's logo solution features a stylized lotus blossom, which in Buddhism represents purity and perfection.

Client: **LaunchIt Public Relations**
San Diego, California, USA

Agency: **Koenig Creative**
San Diego, California

LaunchIt Public Relations is a clever play on words that describes the company's core business: launching products and services. The name inspired this delightful logo, which evokes a paddleball game.

The Challenge

Public relations is an industry devoted to getting new and existing products and services into the public eye via the media. It is a business that rides on instant hit-or-miss communication. A small San Diego–based public relations firm, LaunchIt Public Relations, needed a brand image that addressed its mission: to launch its clients and their wares. Obviously, the company's name is a clever play on words. The firm's brand image had to capture the essence of the agency's playful name while maintaining complete professionalism and the degree of seriousness that appeals to its somewhat conservative client base. The public relations firm also wanted to apply a very limited budget, which required a brand image that could be replicated in two colors.

The Process

It was a rare moment. LaunchIt Public Relations loved the first design presentation! Motion lines and a bouncing red ball to capture of the emotion of action were coupled with the nostalgic vision of a paddleball game—a nearly universal icon that conveys both the client's name and mission.

The Result

The final brand image was applied to LaunchIt Public Relations' stationery and was given life through a clever animated version for its website. The firm has received numerous compliments from both existing and prospective clients.

This action-packed identity bounces and leaps along the company's letterhead and business cards. When the website was designed, the logo was a natural candidate for animation.

The Internet Fund

Resembling an information sign on an interstate highway, Internet Fund's identity tells potential clients the company is well informed about investments and willing to share its knowledge.

Client: **The Internet Fund**
White Plains, New York, USA

Agency: **Langton Cherubino Group, Ltd.**
New York, New York

The Challenge

Langton Cherubino faced a true challenge at the end of the dot-com era. Its client—The Internet Fund—wanted a brand image that conveyed two themes. The first was the Internet, which is associated with growth risk, revolutionary speed, and new opportunities. The second was investment, commonly paired with stability, assets, and long-term returns. The challenge was to reconcile these opposing themes in a world that lost its confidence in Internet investment opportunities.

The Process

The Langton Cherubino design team explored themes of growth and high technology as well as traditional and aggressive investment strategies. The team also concentrated on the client's other dictate: to be seen as the authority on Internet investment while being perceived as a consistently performing resource for financial security. After wallpapering their office with concept sketches, the design team began its exploration by playing with an *i* in a diamond that resembled an interstate highway information sign. The diamond shape then evolved into a variation on the @ symbol.

The Result

The Internet Fund's brand image was employed to launch a marketing campaign that was featured with good success in the *Wall Street Journal, Money* magazine, and dozens of other trade and consumer financial publications. The diamond shape then became the linchpin for a family of fund identities including The Medical Fund and The Internet Fund's parent company, Kinetics Asset Management.

Kinetics Mutual Funds, Inc.

Kinetics Asset Management, Inc.

The **Internet** Fund

The Internet **New Paradigm** Fund

The Internet **Infrastructure** Fund

The Internet **Emerging Growth** Fund

The Internet **Global Growth** Fund

The **Medical** Fund

The **Middle East Growth** Fund

In the promotional materials it becomes evident that Langton Cherubino created such a strong identity that it drives the visuals beyond the logo into a series of subbrands.

The immediate success of Internet Fund's launch led to the development of a family of fund identities, including The Medical Fund and The Internet Fund's parent company, Kinetics Asset Management.

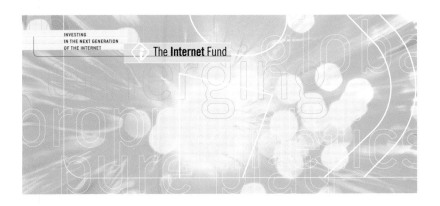

A QUALCOMM® COMPANY

Universal symbology is an essential source of inspiration. Here, radio waves depict communication and bold sans serif italics imply vital motion.

De Run 4413, 5503 LS Veldhoven
P.O. Box 353, 5500 AJ Veldhoven
The Netherlands

Tel: +31 (0) 40 258 24 24
Fax: +31 (0) 76 521 28 93
Web: www.eq-com.nl

PAN-EUROPEAN FLEETMANAGEMENT SOLUTIONS

Floris van Tol
Director
Operations and Purchasing

De Run 4413, 5503 LS Veldhoven
P.O. Box 353, 5500 AJ Veldhoven
The Netherlands

Tel: +31 (0) 40 258 24 24
Fax: +31 (0) 76 521 28 93
E-mail: floris@eq-com.com

PAN-EUROPEAN FLEETMANAGEMENT SOLUTIONS

Client: **Qualcomm Incorporated**
San Diego, California, USA

Agency: **Koenig Creative**
San Diego, California

The Challenge

The establishment of the European Economic Community (EEC) changed the way European companies perceive the globalization of business. Many European firms now prefer to associate themselves with peer businesses rather than American or Asian conglomerates. eQ-COM was formed by the San Diego–based Qualcomm Incorporated as a European company that provides wireless fleet-management solutions to freight transportation companies. The Koenig Creative design team was charged with creating a corporate identity for a company that offered localized pan-European service rather than less personalized long-distance service provided by an American multinational firm. Some elements of the Qualcomm identity had to be incorporated into the final solution. The Koenig Creative design team also had to partner with an Amsterdam-based agency to complete its mission—within a two-month time frame.

The Process

After a quick audit of current European design trends, the Koenig Creative design team offered seven design options. The final design solution was selected because of its simple, italic type treatment that depicted the motion inherent in the client's main business—transportation. The design team selected two elements to depict this business-oriented wireless communication firm: The Q represents the parent company, Qualcomm, and the simple ray motif illustrates the flow of wireless communication. The Amsterdam-based design group contributed the color palette, which features bright green as the statement hue.

The Result

After the eQ-COM brand image was applied to stationery, collateral materials, print advertising, Web presence, trade show booth displays, and presentation materials, the new mark was lauded by the firm's European counterparts, attesting to its international appeal.

PAN-EUROPEAN FLEETMANAGEMENT SOLUTIONS

FutureBrand created a new visual language for the Dopod identity by shaping the logotype from a series of technology-inspired circles.

your world in one

Legibility depends as much on the viewer as the designer. FutureBrand's abstract Dopod logo is readable by the product's target market of tech-savvy consumers.

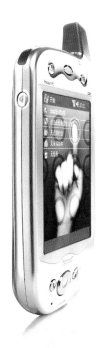

The logo blends seamlessly with the Dopod's buttons to create a futuristic hybrid of organic and tech motion.

Client: **Dopod Communication Corporation**
Shanghai, China

Agency: **FutureBrand, Incorporated**
Singapore, Singapore

The Challenge

A new China-based wireless technology company, Dopod, was geared to launch its namesake revolutionary product—Dopod, the first wireless pocket PC—in the cluttered and competitive consumer technology market when it called on the Singapore branch of FutureBrand to develop its brand image. A technology pioneer that's leading the way in true wireless communications, the company wanted an identity that immediately conveyed keen inspiration, relevance, and premium value to consumers.

The Process

FutureBrand's naming experts created and evaluated more than 300 candidates in an expedited one-month process. The team's search led to the name *Dopod*, which they felt best conveyed the brand's promise to deliver innovation, usability, and activity to its target audience. The final identity derived its inspiration from the backbone of all computer language—binary coding, which uses only *0* and *1* to enumerate all possible combinations. The FutureBrand design team translated this theme using five rings and three dots, symmetrically aligned. The rings also suggest the product's global coverage over five oceans. The *do* at the beginning and end visually imply energy, movement, and dynamism. (In Chinese, this same word means "the way.") The *p* at the name's fulcrum insinuated the word islands that could be readily branded to the product: *phone, platform, pocket PC, portable, play,* and *partner*. Dopod's tagline—"Your world in one"—substantiates the product's placement at the center of the user's universe, providing access to other worlds.

The Result

The FutureBrand design team applied this brand image to the company's stationery and to the premium Dopod 686, which retails for US$986 per unit, for its first offering. The group also implemented the brand on the company's product literature and corporate collateral materials. Last, it developed a comprehensive identity guidelines manual for use in corporate communications and line extension initiatives.

Within six months of its launch, the brand garnered high praise from the technology industry. Even in customer surveys, the brand earned above-average preference over other international brands in the category.

Like a selective mirror, the faces used in the advertising and on the packaging define and attract the target audience.

The extensive use of visual imagery and symbology on the collateral materials reinforces the logo's unique language.

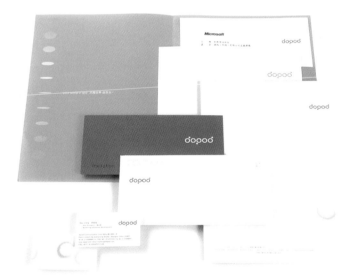

The circular symbols used on the packaging echo the logo itself, increasing the identity's first-sight legibility.

RED SPADE™

Victorian letterpress styling efficiently conveys a human element and a distinct work ethic for Red Spade. The off-center positioning provides additional visual interest while indicating forward motion.

BT-07A-LMSM.live.tif

Client: **Red Spade**
Chicago, Illinois, USA

Agency: **Richard Zeid Design**
Evanston, Illinois

The Challenge

The dot-com era came and went. Far more surprising than the oddball business concepts that failed are the successful companies—the ones that survived. Not only did they have to make it through startup, they also had to overcome the dot-com stigma. It's tough conveying an image of credibility in a post-boom world when your core business consists of providing Web performance audit solutions geared to helping clients improve their online presence. Red Spade identifies effective usability as well as usability gaps that contribute to loss of revenue, customer frustration, and compromised competitive advantage. That's what Richard Zeid Design was charged to do with Red Spade's identity.

The Process

The Richard Zeid design team followed the method employed by Red Spade for developing strategic plans for its own clients. The team researched, vetted, and selected a few names to visually explore. In a second round, the simple iconic image of a red spade was selected for its simplicity, ease of identification, and resonance with a target audience seeking to dig through a mountain of data for answers to marketing problems and building presence in an unsettled environment.

The Result

The simple and elegant solution devised by the design team is the perfect answer to those seeking a no-nonsense firm whose "metrics-driven solutions reveal and address critical usability issues to realize a greater return on your Web-presence investment."

*A multinational conglomer-
ate that markets, processes,
and distributes agricultural
food and financial and
industrial products and
services, Cargill needed a
logo that could be under-
stood in 61 countries.*

Client: **Cargill, Incorporated**
           Wayzata, Minnesota, USA

Agency: **Franke + Fiorella**
           Minneapolis, Minnesota

The Challenge

Cargill is a Minnesota-based multinational conglomerate that markets,
processes, and distributes agricultural food as well as financial and industrial
products and services. Cargill contacted Franke + Fiorella to refresh its identity
by reflecting Cargill's 137-year-long history, its hopes for expansion, and its
existing reach across 61 countries. This was its first review in 36 years.

The Process

After a competitive audit of Cargill's existing identity, collateral materials, signage,
and ancillary applications, the Franke + Fiorella team developed type and color
palettes that reflect the company's agricultural heritage, using a clean, direct
typographic treatment.

The Result

As the client says, "Franke + Fiorella's design solution has been without contro-
versy. It was applauded from the moment it was previewed. It is a forward-look-
ing, friendly design that captures who we are and where we are going. The new
design has made our marketing job easier."

*Franke + Fiorella's identity
program for Cargill includes
printed and online versions
of its guidelines for adapta-
tion by its many subsidiaries
and divisions.*

SCHMIDT &

PETERSON

L I M I T E D

Schmidt & Peterson wanted to position itself as an approachable accounting firm with a nontraditional edge and a professional tone. The juxtaposition of casual illustration and formal type treatment strikes a strong balance.

Client: **Schmidt & Peterson**
Minneapolis, Minnesota, USA

Agency: **Franke + Fiorella**
Minneapolis, Minnesota

The Challenge

The Minneapolis-based accounting firm Schmidt & Peterson wanted to position itself as an approachable resource with a nontraditional edge, speaking in plain English rather than accounting-speak. Franke + Fiorella was given the brief to develop an identity that reflected the company's obvious point of difference while maintaining a professional tone.

The Process

A competitive audit of other tax consultancies and accounting firms was Franke + Fiorella's first stop in the design process. The designers developed a number of concepts, finally settling on a graphic solution. The image centers on a magnified, illustrated view of an adding machine, executed in a black-and-white line drawing style familiar to readers of business publications. Coupled with a traditional-looking serif type treatment, the visual brings together a message of quick comprehension and directness.

The Result

Schmidt & Peterson's new brand successfully sheds the stodgy, bland, unapproachable designs so common with older accounting firm identities.

The accounting firm's stationery system reflects a modern, simple interpretation of the standard professional style.

Once the Graphicwise design team discovered just how fun and easygoing the MousePad corporate culture is, everything fell into place, from the playful hybrid image of a mouse and a computer mouse to the bold color palette.

Client: **MousePad, Inc.**
San Francisco, California, USA

Agency: **Graphicwise**
Irvine, California

The Challenge

There is a fine line between fun, engaging, approachable design and cartoonish visuals that won't instill confidence in clients. This northern California–based company wanted its identity to welcome technological neophytes. The trick was to make the symbol of the mouse as unique and memorable as possible while maintaining the balance between entertaining and professional imagery.

The Process

Graphicwise's initial designs were far too structured and professional, erring safely away from playful graphics. But once the team discovered just how fun and easygoing the company's corporate culture is, everything fell into place. With the name MousePad, Graphicwise toyed with images of mice and computer-related equipment. The winner turned out to be an abstract hybrid of animal mouse and computer mouse with a mouse pad background.

The Result

The lighthearted identity opened the door for other creative design solutions. For example, each employee's business card is personalized with his or her image in silhouette.

200 market street, suite 850
san francisco, ca 94111

415 . 970 . 8850
415 . 970 . 8855

innovative people need
innovative software

sharon h. wang
sr. software developer

direct line: 415 . 970 . 8897
email: swang@mousepad.com
address: 200 market street, #850
   san francisco, ca 94111
hobbies: gardening

A fanciful, concrete silhouette adds life to each MousePad employee's business card. Besides conventional information, each card also lists the person's hobbies.

MousePad's curved-corner letterhead takes its shape from computer mouse pads.

The HADW design team discovered that in the world of web analysis and marketing products, the letter Q stands for the Q-sorting method, a practical means of sorting and analyzing large forms of data.

aQuantive

Client: **aQuantive**
Seattle, Washington, USA

Agency: **Hornall Anderson Design Works, Inc.**
Seattle, Washington

The Challenge

aQuantive, Inc., is the parent company of one of the industry's most successful digital marketing families; Avenue A and i-Frontier are interactive marketing agencies, and Atlas DMT develops tools for delivering effective digital marketing campaigns. Founded in 1997, the Seattle-based aQuantive helps global companies tap into online media's incredible marketing power, enabling marketers to reach one of the world's fastest-growing segments—the online customer. According to Jupiter Research 1, an online market research firm, online advertising expenditures in the United States grew to $6.2 billion in 2003 and will grow to $14 billion by 2007, outpacing TV, print, and radio. The company needed a new brand identity that reflected its growth in this rapidly expanding industry and called on Hornall Anderson Design Works, Inc. (HADW), to develop a new look and feel.

The Process

The HADW design team discovered that in the world of Web analysis and marketing products, the letter *Q* stands for the Q-sorting method, a practical means of sorting and analyzing large forms of data. Stressing the *Q* in aQuantive's name points to a major service it provides its clients. The broken serif letterform is enhanced in blue.

The Result

The hidden strength in this brand is its distinctive letter *Q*. Split into a stencil style, it takes on a parenthetical or encompassing quality—perfect for a parent company that embraces its subsidiaries.

aQuantive's business cards employ familiar visual elements associated with computers and analysis: binary code, bar codes, and abstract units.

Stressing the Q in aQuantive's name points to the major service the company provides its clients—Q-sorting—and is enhanced as a standalone blue icon on the company's letterhead.

ORIV●

Orivo revitalizes brands that were not previously reaching their potential. Its logo needed to look established and solid with a timeless, European flair.

Client: **Orivo**
Seattle, Washington, USA

Agency: **Hornall Anderson Design Works, Inc.**
Seattle, Washington

The Challenge

Orivo is a Seattle-based company that sells ideas. Founded by David Sinegal, the company revitalizes brands by licensing brands that had not been reaching their potential and relicensing them. It also extends brands into new markets by identifying untapped opportunities. When Orivo launched its operation in 2002, it called on Hornall Anderson Design Works (HADW) to create a clean, simple, timeless identity with a European flair. The challenge faced by HADW was that Orivo didn't want to look like a startup company despite its newness. It needed to look established and solid.

The Process

Rather than researching graphic symbols and other illustrative elements that would detract from Orivo's business position, the HADW team directed its attention to the creation of a dynamic but noninvasive presence. A strong type-only design solution was the result; it combines a striking lowercase, sans serif type treatment with a rich red palette.

The Result

HADW's design solution was an important part of the accolades Orivo received, including a Silver Northwest Addy Award for the design of their latest brochure.

A dynamic, noninvasive presence, the Orivo logo derives its strength from its striking uppercase type treatment and the contrast between the first and last letters of its name.

On its collateral materials, the Orivo O becomes a repetitive motif that conveys a simple message: The company turns dreams into reality.

Client: **Scotchprint Graphics**
St. Paul, Minnesota, USA

Agency: **Franke + Fiorella**
Minneapolis, Minnesota

The Challenge

The Scotchprint Graphics brand name had been established for more than 20 years when the 3M Company's Commercial Graphics Division called on Franke + Fiorella to create its brand image. Scotchprint Graphics, which employs 3M products to generate custom application graphics for vehicles, buildings, floors, walls, banners, and any other place giant signage can be affixed, had a loyal commercial following. Consequently, the design team had to develop visual branding that resonated with the target's current brand perceptions while enhancing its image for future line extensions.

The commercial graphics division of 3M Company, the Scotchprint Graphics brand, had built strong equity over the course of 20 years with a loyal customer base. The new identity not only reinforced current brand perceptions but also paved the way for future line extensions.

The Process

The Franke + Fiorella design team executed an extensive competitive audit before conducting extensive research and exploring a number of design options. They selected a bright poster-paint palette paired with a bold san-serif type treatment.

The Result

In addition to implementing the solution across all of the division's communications, the team also developed an animated soundmark for use in the product line's electronic media presentations and software splash screens.

The Scotchprint Graphics brand's bright poster-paint palette and bold type treatment are prominently featured across all their materials, creating a consistent and memorable campaign.

StorageNetworking.org

Founded by the Information Storage Industry Center (ISIC) at UCSD, StorageNetworking.org offers online support data storage technology user groups. Its logo demonstrates the company's ability to point the way within a well-organized structure.

Client: **University of California, San Diego**
San Diego, California, USA

Agency: **Koenig Creative**
San Diego, California

The Challenge

Over the past decade, the information storage, retrieval, and distribution business has exceeded the confines of file folders, storage cabinets, and warehouses. StorageNetworking.org was founded by the Information Storage Industry Center (ISIC) at University of California, San Diego, with a grant from the Storage Networking Industry Association (SNIA) and the Sloan Foundation to support data storage technology usergroups so users can interact with their peers and other experts about this critical industry. The biggest design challenge the Koenig Creative team faced was the length of the organization's name, which had to be incorporated into a logo without abbreviation.

The Process

The Koenig Creative team developed several identity concepts. Each conveyed a different visual representation of technology and personal networking. The final logo was chosen based on its simple typographic treatment. The use of the letter *o* in the name depicts separate disks or nodes, and the flowchart line elements represent their interconnection.

The Result

The StorageNetworking.org site is currently being beta tested. Both the logo and the website design have been well received by the client and the site sponsors, who particularly like the design's simplicity and the way logo elements carry through the site.

StorageNetworking.org

University of California, San Diego
9500 Gilman Drive
La Jolla, CA 92093-0519
Telephone (858) 534-9825
Fax (858) 534-3939
E-mail: isic@ucsd.edu

Supporting the Users
of Data Storage Technology

The two-color tagline at the bottom of the letterhead supports the logo. The letter o in the company's name depicts a disk or node, while the flowchart line elements represent the interconnection of the nodes.

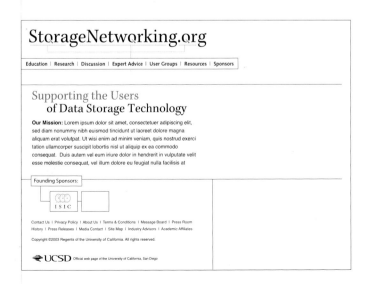

Accordis's logo incorporates
an organic curve sweeping
through a triangle that
depicts accord between
the two distinctly different
shapes and creates the
letter A—the first letter in
the company's name.

Client: **The Kudelski Group/Accordis Technologies**
San Diego, California, USA

Agency: **Koenig Creative**
San Diego, California

The Challenge

The Kudelski Group is an international company that operates a number of varied
technology subsidiaries providing integrated security systems for both digital
television and broadband networks, including digital decoders and encoders for
integrated management systems used in event venues. Until recently, each subsidiary
had a distinct corporate identity that lacked continuity with its parent organization.
Most of these brands were dated, having been created during the 1980s.

A recent Kudelski Group acquisition, Accordis Technologies, was a startup business
specializing in the development of set-top cable box technology. Koenig Creative
was commissioned to develop an identity that stood alone from other Kudelski
brands but clearly conveyed its own message: a global player that creates technologies that integrate seamlessly with other set-top systems.

The Process

The Koenig Creative team explored numerous solutions, including several that
visualized the concept of harmony. Experimentation with simple Zen symbols—
squares, a circle, and a triangle—and the letter O focused on illustrating
Accordis's desire for integration with other systems. The solution incorporated
an organic curve sweeping through a triangle, depicting accord between the
two distinctly different shapes and creating the letter A—the first letter in the
company's name. The curve was repeated as design element in the company's
stationery kit.

The Result

The final Accordis Technologies logo garnered high praise from both the client
and its European parent, Kudelski Group. The identity was applied to stationery,
collateral, and package branding, and the product will be launched in 2004.

The sweeping curve in
Accordis's iconic letter A is
echoed in a sweeping curve
at the base of its letterhead.

Accordis Technologies specializes in the development
of set-top cable box technology, and its logo is
branded on each of its
products, such as the one
shown here.

For Cosmic Sumo's identity, Matthew Walker created a caricature of a sumo wrestler by drawing a 1950s cartoon-style face. He looked to the same era for his typeface selection.

CosmicSumo.com
New York, New York, USA

Walk Design
Rocky Hill, Connecticut, USA

The Challenge

CosmicSumo.com was developed as a community-based website where online viewers could find a hodgepodge of information. The website's business and goals were still being formulated when Matthew Walker was called in to create its identity. The biggest challenge the designer faced was that the name really didn't mean anything. "The logo was really fun to design because I had so much freedom," Walker explains. "But the freedom made it very difficult as well. It's hard to manage and live up to a client's expectation when the goals and the strategies aren't there."

The Process

Walker did some basic research on sumo history and found that too daunting for the target audience. So he decided to create a caricature of a sumo wrestler by drawing a 1950s cartoon-style face. He looked to the same era for his typeface selection and presented the solution with three different type treatments.

The Result

A strong, content-rich site was built around the look and feel of Walker's logo. The logo was used primarily for the website and secondarily for its stationery program.

The 1950s motif is emphasized by the ellipital knock-out on the front of the business cards and the atomic symbols on both sides.

Which came first? In this case, the logo was created before the website and heavily influenced the site's design and content.

agere systems

The Agere Systems identity, designed to stand out among predominantly blue-hued tech-oriented logos, was completed in 12 weeks and launched in 120 countries.

Client: **Agere Systems**
Allentown, Pennsylvania, USA

Agency: **Lippincott Mercer**
New York, New York, USA

The Challenge

Agere Systems is a premier provider of advanced integrated-circuit solutions for wireless data, high-density storage, and multiservice networking applications. The company is a market leader whose 67 facilities worldwide include design and application centers, sales offices, and manufacturing units. This technology-oriented operation commissioned Lippincott Mercer to develop a refreshed brand identity that reflected its numerous interests. The new identity needed to launch in 120 countries—but the real challenge was the schedule. The entire brand program had to be completed in 12 weeks.

The Process

The Lippincott Mercer development team worked hand in hand with the client to select more than 1,300 names and follow through preliminary legal, linguistic, and URL screenings to identify the best candidate. The team then crafted a focused brand-positioning statement through extensive executive and customer interviews, a competitive audit, and review of media/analyst reports. Logotypes, symbols, and wordmarks for five finalist concepts were concurrently produced for client presentation.

The Result

The selected logo and design system uses a multitiered, lowercase type treatment executed against a stark white backdrop to differentiate Agere Systems in its highly competitive, predominantly blue-hued marketplace. Lippincott Mercer designed and produced the launch kit materials for Agere Systems' launch at its worldwide sales conference. The agency also created online guidelines with downloadable templates for ease of implementation on marketing collateral, presentations, sales materials, and signage.

When the logo is emblazoned on a CD and CD case, it becomes apparent that the design is not low tech but, rather, a different perspective on technology.

The minimalist typographic logo set the clean tone for Agere Systems' collateral materials, which were also created by Lippincott Mercer.

Client: **ChevronTexaco**
San Ramon, California, USA

Agency: **Lippincott Mercer**
New York, New York, USA

ChevronTexaco

When Chevron and Texaco merged, Lippincott Mercer incorporated qualities of each company, discovered through extensive research, into a proprietary typeface.

The Challenge

Two energy giants—Chevron and Texaco—united forces in 2001, becoming the world's fourth largest publicly traded integrated energy company and the second largest in the United States. Active in over 180 countries worldwide, the conglomerate employs about 53,000 employees, not including service station staffs. Ideally, a brand development agency is called early in the process to assure that the newly formed organization presents a strong mission statement, well-stated goals, and solid supporting brand messages to both investors and the public. Lippincott Mercer was approached late in this vital process and was given a tight deadline for the completion of the visual solution, hundreds of applications, and corresponding guidelines.

The Process

An audit revealed that the merging companies were each represented by more than a single image. There were myriad colors, supporting symbols, and type treatments. To facilitate research and discovery, the Lippincott Mercer design team gathered the entire collection of elements and crafted a matrix of the logo equities. More than an excellent presentation tool, the matrix brought to light numerous possibilities for merging and/or emphasizing facets of each company's identity during the conceptualization phase. The ultimate solution called for the creation of a proprietary typeface containing characteristics that resonate with the combined companies' existing investors, target audiences, and prospective consumers.

The Result

The enormous applications program included applying the mark to brochures, magazines, stationery and signage systems, a marketing collateral system, a website (www.chevrontexaco.com), and awards. Lippincott Mercer also created printed and online guidelines with downloadable templates for ChevronTexaco's numerous international offices and licensees.

To maintain the integrity of the logotype, the logo font is reserved for the brand name rather than carrying over into other headings in the company's extensive collateral materials.

HOUSEHOLD

In an industry characterized by big, featureless banking corporations, Household's accessible icon brings a warm, human face to America's second largest issuer of private-label credit cards.

Client: **Household**
Prospect Heights, Illinois, USA

Agency: **Lippincott Mercer**
New York, New York, USA

The Challenge

Household International is a $123 billion provider of consumer loan, credit card, auto finance, and credit insurance products in the United States, the United Kingdom, and Canada. Serving the financial needs of middle-market consumers since 1878, Household now serves more than 50 million people in all three nations and offers a broad set of financial products and services. The company ranks as the eighth largest issuer of MasterCard and Visa credit cards. Household is America's second largest issuer of private-label credit cards. In the United Kingdom and Canada, the company also provides auto finance, tax refund lending, retail funding, and insurance products to its consumer and business clients.

The Process

The Lippincott Mercer design team was contracted to explore, present, and implement a brand image that could encompass all of Household's services and multinational target markets. The team developed a wide range of design solutions that included logotypes, wordmarks, and symbols. After the client approved the concept, the team tested the logo against the positioning and image attributes in extensive research. The solution employs a clean, confident type treatment and a red earth color palette.

The Result

The enhanced visibility and improved perception of the new Household entity contributed to its acquisition in 2002 by HSBC as a key component of the latter's expansion into the United States. Headquartered in London, HSBC Holdings PLC is one of the world's largest banking and financial services organizations, with more than 9,500 offices in 79 countries.

Household's collateral materials extend the humanness through the use of illustrative and photographic images of real people.

The logo's colors create a warm palette that's rare in the financial world's sea of blues, grays, and greens.

¯TUNGSTEN™

Tungsten's dynamic red and gray logo demands attention from its discerning audience of mobile professionals and businesspeople.

Client: **palmOne, Inc./Tungsten**
Milpitas, California, USA

Agency: **Turner Duckworth**
San Francisco, California; and London, UK

The Challenge

Because Tungsten had to live alongside palmOne's Zire logo and appeal to a different audience, its brand image needed to incorporate both clear similarities and strong differences. Unlike Zire's general consumer and multimedia target base and Treo's smartphone audience, the Tungsten targeted a very special and very demanding audience: mobile professionals and businesses who rely on these wireless, handheld communication devices.

The Process

The Turner Duckworth design team worked with palmOne to create a concise creative brief before developing a handful of significantly different designs. As with all of Turner Duckworth's projects, this work in progress was sent to the San Francisco office's London sister office for a serious critique. The London team helped the team edit and improve the concepts before they were shown to the client. The selected logo did not change after the initial presentation. In fact, as with the Zire design, the client canceled the team's research phase because they were so sure this was the right answer.

The Result

The final Tungsten brand image employs a strong sans serif type treatment and a red and gray palette that complements the parent company's red and gold color scheme. The logo appears on the division's products, packaging, the palmOne website, advertising, and all marketing materials. The Tungsten brand allowed palmOne to successfully target specific products at demanding mobile and professional users.

Able to stand alongside its parent logo—palmOne—the Tungsten identity maintains its point of difference on the product itself and its website.

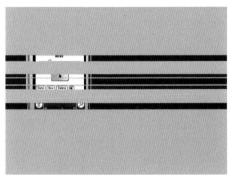

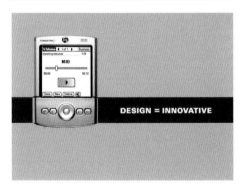

The red lines that provide the focal point of Tungsten's logo also serve as a binding element when animated for the Web.

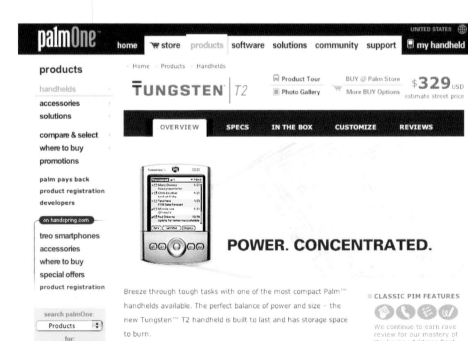

palmOne™

A radical departure of its original color scheme, palmOne's new identity stands out in a sea of blues and grays, allowing for a broader, more dynamic range of future brand extensions under a red and gold palette.

Client: **palmOne, Inc.**
Milpitas, California, USA

Agency: **Turner Duckworth**
San Francisco, California; and London, UK

The Challenge

Palm, Inc., made a name for itself in the 1990s as a leading manufacturer of handheld computers and smartphones. Its PalmSource division became the largest and most respected developer and licenser of the Palm OS platform. In 2003, the company acquired another industry leader, Handspring, Inc., and made plans to spin off PalmSource as a separate company. The move triggered the need to create a new brand identity, palmOne, Inc.

Designers of the original Palm logo, Turner Duckworth, had recently finished developing the imagery for palmOne's subbrands Tungsten and Zire (see pages 55 and 58) when the team was commissioned to create the new palmOne identity program.

The Process

Based in San Francisco, the Turner Duckworth team developed several concepts that underwent scrutiny by its London sister agency before they were presented to the client. In addition to this process, the team created a special presentation intended to encourage palmOne to abandon its existing blue palette for a bolder red range that tied in with the Tungsten and Zire subbrand palettes. The presentation demonstrated how many of palmOne's competitors employed blue palettes. It also pointed out how other companies in other markets have successfully employed distinctive color combinations as a useful point of difference. (PalmSource has retained the original blue color scheme.)

The Result

PalmOne's condensed type treatment, with its red and gold palette, is being introduced on the company's product lines and packaging. It already offers a distinctive visual presence on its website, collateral materials, and a bold print ad campaign. The new palmOne logo and its applications have helped the company and its acquisition, Handspring, make a successful transition with both investors and consumers.

palmOne

Desktop Software

Turner Duckworth's design for palmOne makes a strong statement not only on its website and print ad campaign, it even presents a strong face on the products themselves and on software packaging, as seen here.

PalmOne's red and gold image is complemented by its subbrand Zire's silver and orange identity.

PalmOne's new identity stands apart from the competition, even when translated across numerous languages and continents and on the Web.

Please select your destination.

North America
- Canada
- United States

Africa
- Region

Middle East
- Region

Europe
- Region
- Austria
- Belgium-English
- Belgium-French
- Denmark
- Eastern Europe
- Finland
- France
- Germany
- Ireland
- Italy
- Luxembourg
- Mediterranean
- The Netherlands
- Norway
- Spain
- Sweden
- Switzerland-French
- Switzerland-German
- UK

Asia Pacific
- Region
- Australia
- China
- Hong Kong-English
- Hong Kong-Chinese
- India
- Japan
- Malaysia
- New Zealand
- Philippines
- Singapore
- Taiwan-English
- Taiwan-Chinese
- Thailand

Latin America
- Region
- Argentina
- Brazil
- Chile
- Colombia
- Mexico
- Peru
- Venezuela

Zire™

The Zire logo's message of simplicity and accessibility is evident even when it appears with the palmOne identity on the company's website.

Client: **palmOne, Inc.**
Milpitas, California, USA

Agency: **Turner Duckworth**
San Francisco, California; and London, UK

The Challenge

Zire had the dubious honor of being launched while its parent company was in a major transition phase. A subbrand of palmOne, the Zire handheld computer targets general consumers and multimedia enthusiasts. The product's logo had to be dynamic enough to appeal to an entertainment-oriented, not-so-tech-savvy, youthful market in numerous media, including as an animated identity on the company's website.

The Process

The San Francisco Turner Duckworth design team worked hand in hand with its London-based office to develop a handful of distinctive concepts, employing a sleek sans serif type treatment and a silver and orange palette that complements the parent company's red and gold color scheme. The chosen logo did not change after the initial presentation; the client canceled the research phase because they were confident of the solution.

The Result

The final brand image is used on products, packaging, the website, advertising, and all marketing materials. It even showed up on a fleet of branded Parisian taxis. The Zire brand allowed palmOne to successfully target new customers: ordinary consumers who are not tech savvy. Consequently, the first Zire product was the fastest-selling handheld in the company's history.

Appealing to an entertainment-oriented, not-so-tech-savvy, youthful market, Zire's color palette and accent elements translate into a promise of fun when animated for the Web.

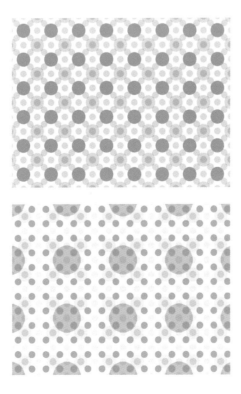

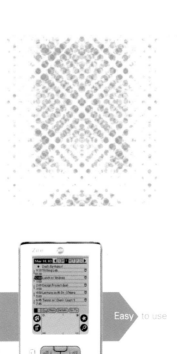

Client: **Heavenly**
London, UK

Agency: **Turner Duckworth**
San Francisco, California, USA; and London, UK

The Challenge

Heavenly is a marketing consultancy that specializes in down-to-earth thinking for its clients. The firm's name—the opposite of its nature—posed a challenge to Turner Duckworth when it was called in to create Heavenly's brand identity.

The Process

The fun part of working on this project was the name's brain-teasing dilemma, especially after the Turner Duckworth design team resisted the urge to employ cliché heavenly imagery. This meant no halos, angel wings, fluffy clouds, biblical references, or spiritual typefaces. They arrived at the solution by playing word games, including "heavenly" as part of a statement. "Heavenly: a nice cup of tea" eventually led to "Heavenly...down-to-earth thinking." At that point, the word shed its physical and religious meanings and became an emotive descriptor, allowing the team to revisit the name without the baggage. Not an easy job, but very rewarding.

The designers dove in, using Helvetica Bold for the type treatment. The graphic plays on the eye. Initially, it appears that a star is coming down from the sky under the letter *h*. On second viewing, a hidden arrow appears in the negative space between the letter and the star. The tagline—"down-to-earth thinking"—always appears with the mark.

The Result

Turner Duckworth's clean and straightforward logo employs a tactic similar to the FedEx mark—a hidden arrow in the negative space. This bold new mark is as striking when used in full as when it is used more minimally with just the *h* and the star.

heavenly™

Heavenly's name posed a real challenge for Turner Duckworth. The design team had to find non-cliché elements to present a strong message for this marketing consultancy that specializes in down-to-earth thinking for its clients.

An arrow created in the negative space between the letter h and the star points to Heavenly's feet-on-the-ground approach to the tactics and strategies it develops for its clients.

UK online

The Interbrand design team discovered the mainstream British public is strongly attracted to bright, colorful palettes during its exploration phase of the UK Online identity.

UK Online's bright, refreshed identity offers an accessible, youthful message when applied to product packaging, as seen here.

Client: **UK Online/Easynet**
Somerset, UK

Agency: **Interbrand**
London, UK

The Challenge
The United States isn't the only country where Internet technology and Web surfing have exploded into the mainstream. In the United Kingdom, UK Online/Easynet was a pioneer service provider, and it continues to be a major player in this highly competitive industry. UK Online's expanding scope of business demanded refreshment and evolution of the company's identity. The Interbrand team was called in to breathe new life into the brand while keeping it populist, accessible, bright, and dynamic in the eyes of its youth-oriented market. The main problem the creative team faced was how to retain some element of the original brand's Britishness without being too blatant.

The Process
Restraint is often associated with British culture. In their logo solution, the Interbrand team employed popular British imagery—the Houses of Parliament and Big Ben—in the *on* portion of the logotype—with the appropriate amount of restraint. Through the brand strategy development process, the team discovered the British public is strongly attracted to bright and colorful palettes, which it associates with friendliness and accessibility.

The Result
UK Online is in the process of implementing the final identity, which will soon appear throughout all communications applications, from stationery and collateral materials to its website (www.ukonline.net) and the packaging of its ISP services, which include broadband, unlimited dialup, pay-as-you-surf, entertainment, news, and shopping services. The new mark, with its rounded type treatment and London skyline, is both approachable and memorable, sure to distinguish the company among competitors.

UK online broadband
UK online broadband

welcome to the fastest, most reliable and easy
to install broadband service in the UK

Bright, youthful, and dynamic are the statements made by UK Online's identity program when translated into the various components of its website.

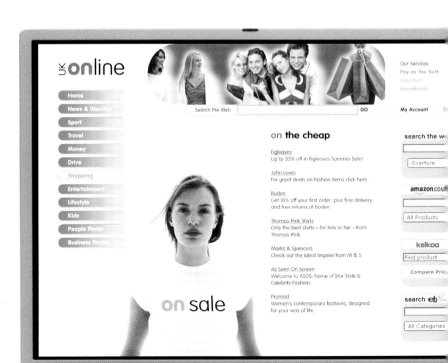

Trust Investment Bank's brand identity cleverly combines Russian and English influences in a simple and discreet image. The two Ts in the word TRUST point the way business expands out of the RUS, which stands for the institution's Russian clientele.

Client: **Trust Investment Bank**
Moscow, Russia

Agency: **Interbrand**
London, UK

The Challenge

After decades of isolation from the capitalist world, Russia is emerging as a vital new economic force filled with opportunities, optimism, and enthusiasm. Like every nation that has entered the global playing field in the last 20 years, Russia has relied on both domestic and international investors for growth. The Trust Investment Bank is one such clearinghouse for the financial resources Russian-based businesses need to succeed. Interbrand was called in to create a brand that would reflect the level of confidence, professionalism, and integrity investors, borrowers, and consumers expect from an investment bank no matter where it's located.

With promises of optimism, opportunity, enthusiasm, and potential economic growth, Trust Investment Bank's identity also conveys confidence, professionalism, and integrity.

The Process

The Interbrand design team went through a four-stage process to create Trust Investment Bank's brand. At first, the team developed brand strategy through extensive research and survey. They then developed design concepts based on that accumulated information. The development and implementation stages, which included focus grouping of a variety of solutions, helped both the team and the client realize the final candidate's potential for use across a broad range of media. The selected brand identity cleverly combines Russian and English influences in a simple and discreet image. The two T's in the word *TRUST* point the way business expands out of the *RUS*, which stands for the institution's Russian clientele.

The Result

Trust Investment Bank's new identity, with its sophisticated and forward-thinking look, was implemented in 2003 across the range of the company's business applications, from its brand book and corporate brochure to its stationery and website (www.trust.ru). The company's brand and its core business have met with rave reviews in Russia; surely the memorable logo has something to do with this.

Launched in 2003, Trust Investment Bank's logo has met with rave reviews in Russia, where it's seen on the company's signage and website.

Royal Bank of Canada's expansion into the United States called for a refreshed identity that would resonate with both loyal Canadian consumers and potential American clients who knew nothing of the brand's equity as Canada's leading financial service provider.

Client: **Royal Bank of Canada**
Toronto, Ontario, Canada

Agency: **FutureBrand**
New York, New York, USA; and Toronto, Ontario

The Challenge

Royal Bank of Canada, Canada's leading financial services provider, has the distinction of owning the brand with the highest unaided awareness in the nation. The first financial institution to take advantage of the North American Fair Trade Agreement (NAFTA), Royal Bank of Canada acquired a number of financial institutions in the United States. Its initial purchase was Centura Bank, a personal and commercial banking operation located in the Southeast. This cross-border expansion called for a refreshed identity that would resonate with consumers in both Canada and the United States. FutureBrand's challenge was to create a brand that encompassed the institution's core services as well as its new holdings without losing its equity with its loyal client base. To achieve the most effective results, FutureBrand teams in New York and Toronto collaborated throughout the process.

The Process

In its initial research, the FutureBrand team discovered that perceptions of Royal Bank's identity differed greatly in the United States from those found in its Canadian homeland. The surveyed U.S. market was unwilling to accept the concept of banking with a Canadian bank. The same target group also rejected the idea of banking at an institution with the word *royal* in its name.

The FutureBrand team created an initialism that stood for Royal Bank of Canada's heritage: RBC. The initialism was then applied to each of the bank's key services, including RBC Centura, RBC Builder Finance, RBC Financial Group, RBC Investments, RBC Mortgages, and RBC Capital Markets. The FutureBrand team then modernized the institution's lion and globe symbol—last updated in the early 1960s—so it could be used with greater impact in print, broadcast, and Internet treatments.

In focus groups, Americans rejected the idea of banking at an institution with the word royal *in its name, so the FutureBrand team created an initialism that stood for the financial institution's strong heritage and allowed for line extensions to each of its key services.*

The Result

FutureBrand's New York– and Toronto-based teams used the modernized icon to create a set of RBC-branded core competencies/platforms for use in Canada as well as a set of RBC-led cobrands for use in the United States. The significant brand revitalization program, introduced by RBC's new chair, launched the massive repositioning program across North America. RBC's identity update was well accepted in Canada; consumers were happy that RBC was keeping up with the times by creating a fresh look for the company without losing the equity it had accumulated over 150 years. Financial institutions that transitioned to RBC have also been well received by consumers in the United States.

RBC's rebranding was well accepted in Canada. Consumers were happy that RBC was keeping up with the times by creating a fresh look for the company without losing its 150-year-long equity.

Client: **Oi**
Rio de Janiero, Brazil

Agency: **Wolff Olins**
London, UK

*To gain share in a market-
place packed with 20
competing services
providers, Oi presents a
cool, casual, conversant
persona to its audience. Oi
means "hi" in Portuguese.*

The Challenge

Anywhere but Brazil, the Brazilian mobile phone market would be perceived
as saturated. The country already had 20 competing service providers when
Oi entered the marketplace. Wolff Olins was commissioned to discover a
visual expression that would stand out in the marketplace, provide a point of
difference in an arena dominated by players offering complicated products
and using bureaucratic language.

The Process

Since the majority of Oi's competitors offered a formal and corporate presence,
the Wolff Olins team chose a cool, casual, and human approach to their solution. In Portuguese, the word oi means "hi." From that starting point, the team
searched for typographic, color, and visual treatments that would convey the
message across the board.

The Result

The brand identity created by Wolff Olins was implemented consistently across a
wide range of applications including stationery, advertising, point-of-sale graphics,
and promotional items. Wolff Olins also designed Oi's phone packaging and retail
sites. Oi reached one million customers in only five months of existence, and
75 percent of its new clients left its competitors. The Oi brand identity was a
finalist in the 2003 International Design 7 Effectiveness Awards as well as in the
2003 London International Advertising Awards. The Brazilian equivalent of the
Economist magazine, *Istoe Dinheiro*, called Oi's success "a phenomenon." In
Brazil, the word *Oi* has replaced the word *cellular* in current vernacular. Two Oi
fan clubs and an Oi chat room have been created.

*It's a testament to the
power of simplicity. The
word Oi has replaced the
word cellular in current
Brazilian vernacular. The
company gained a million
customers in its first five
months, thanks to its youthful and human approach.*

*Much like Apple's clamshell
iBook design, Oi's design
and packaging presents a
welcome contrast to the
competition's high-tech
identities, which frequently
intimidate new consumers.*

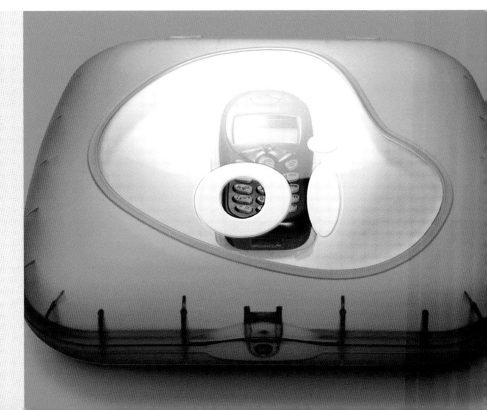

LIVEBYTES
Video Communication Solutions

Client: **Livebytes, Inc.**
Aliso Viejo, California, USA

Agency: **Mark McLaughlin**
San Diego, California

The Challenge

Documents and still images were once the only forms that traveled on the Internet or from computer to computer. More and more, video is transferred from one location to another between consumers, consumers and businesses, and between businesses. Often, some level of privacy is desired. Sometimes it's paramount. Livebytes developed a technology that conveys video through secure systems. The company wanted a brand identity to broadcast that message to its core audience: government offices and corporate security departments. The logo had to convey an impression of constant motion, whether it appeared in online media or in print. The challenge Mark McLaughlin faced was to convey confidence and security in that same image.

The Process

McLaughlin explored several symbols that communicate either movement or security. He then developed a grid of small orange shapes that narrowed to a fine point, creating a sense of energy and motion. Four monitors rotate around each other in a rectangular formation, connected by the orange "energy effects." The finished image symbolizes a wall of protection in which energy can freely flow.

The Result

The identity gained strong response within three months of its launch. The technology company's sales manager has referred to the logo as a sales piece in and of itself. It has also been a topic of conversation raised by prospective clients referred from Livebyte's website.

Security software developer Livebytes' icon consists of four monitors that rotate around each other, expressing a flow of digital energy protected by a wall of security.

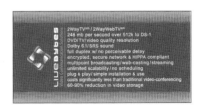

The edge treatments of Livebytes' stationery are dynamic complements to the active logo itself.

*Clearpoint's logo offers
employers and jobseekers a
clear highway to success:
Two roads converge and
move upward, forming a
definitive point.*

Client: **Clearpoint Solutions**
             La Jolla, California, USA

Agency: **Mark McLaughlin**
             San Diego, California

The Challenge

Recruiting firms like Clearpoint Solutions do more than find people jobs.
Recruitment begins by establishing relationships with companies that, inevitably,
need to seek people to fill available positions. The process continues by identifying an individual's talents, skills, and potential, and then finding a position in
which those elements can grow and thrive. Clearpoint Solutions felt that both the
employer and employee had to be represented in its brand and identified Mark
McLaughlin as the man for the job.

The Process

McLaughlin employed his own talent and skills to develop a concept that reinforced Clearpoint Solution's mission to help each employer successfully acquire
the best person for each job and to help each employee experience true
achievement. After experimenting with a number of shapes and concepts, he
discovered that two roads converging and moving upward together to a definitive point—the clearpoint—best communicated this message.

The Result

The client's feedback has been extremely positive. The company has established
itself as a high-end staffing firm with strong brand recognition and measurable
growth: Clearpoint Solutions has grown over 300 percent since the brand identity's inception.

Christopher J. Page
Managing Partner

4275 Executive Square   T 858.373.2516
              Suite 318   D 619.981.3632
          La Jolla, CA 92037   F 858.455.0157
clearpointsolutionsinc.com   cpage@clearpointsolutionsinc.com

*At center stage on a business
card, the new logo evokes
upward mobility—key to
establishing client trust.*

Consumer Explorers' identity strongly conveys the message that the company gets to the core of marketing strategies through creative consumer research that spells profits for its clients.

Adages about consumers reinforce the brand's message on Consumer Explorers' game card–like business cards.

Client: **Consumer Explorers**
New York, New York, USA

Agency: **98pt6**
New York, New York

The Challenge

Consumer Explorers is an intelligent, intuitive, creative consumer research company. Highly imaginative and insightful in its approach, the company is frequently contracted by large clients such as corporations and ad agencies to validate or discover marketing strategies that could generate millions of dollars. The logo had to capture the company's creativity without sacrificing the bearing and appearance needed to negotiate in the corporate arena. Therein lay the difficulty for 98pt6, the brand essence company hired to develop the logo.

The Process

To create the perfect brand identity, the 98pt6 team convened a group of the best consumer researchers they knew and conducted creative, brainstorming exercises. From these, they arrived at a few thought-provoking visual metaphors for truth and the consumer observation process. The result: The logo's green apple, bitten to the core, is set against backdrops in lively hues.

The Result

Though reminiscent of Seymour Chwast's classic illustrative work and color palette, the final result is utterly contemporary and memorable.

A strong, bright palette accompanies Consumer Explorers' green apple, accentuating the silhouetted profiles formed at the icon's core.

GORE•TEX®

Client: **Gore-Tex Fabrics**
Newark, Delaware, USA

Agency: **Bergman Associates**
New York, New York, USA

The Challenge

Introduced around 30 years ago, Gore-Tex revolutionized performance outer-wear. This miraculous fabric allows moisture to escape but repels rain and blocks wind, keeping wearers warm and dry in all sorts of inclement weather. Gore-Tex outerwear quickly became an essential wardrobe component for every-one from inveterate adventurers to suburban soccer moms.

Gore-Tex fabric is available only to a limited number of better outerwear manu-facturers, and every item made with Gore-Tex fabric carries the Gore-Tex brand. Thus, it has become a seal of quality to consumers. Bergman Associates' chal-lenge was to bring this classic logo up to date and to build on its hard-earned reputation.

The Process

Bergman Associates took cues from Gore-Tex's familiar wide, san-serif type treatment, slimming its appearance with an extra-black condensed font. The brand's signature red arrow was replaced by a vocabulary of five icons that explain the fabric's qualities and the company's registered tagline, "Guaranteed to Keep You Dry."

The Result

The new, robust Gore-Tex brand—in both a stand-alone typographic version and an iconic-complement version—is a radical improvement over and significant change from the previous mark. Nevertheless, it has such a timeless and appro-priate feel that consumers are likely to think the brand looked like that all along.

The Gore-Tex logo has become a seal of quality to consumers. Its refreshed image is significantly stronger than its predecessor, implying guaranteed pro-tection from the elements.

Building on its hard-earned reputation, the Gore-Tex identity includes a vocabu-lary of five icons that explain the fabric's qualities and the company's registered tagline: "Guaranteed to Keep You Dry."

DEEP SEA MINING TECHNOLOGY

A morph of waves and mining drills expresses the core of Descent's business: the little known but rapidly expanding deep-sea mining industry.

Client: **Descent**
Belfast, Northern Ireland

Agency: **The Missive**
New York, New York, USA

The Challenge

Demand for metals and minerals increases year by year. Meanwhile, land-bound resources are diminishing, paving the way for the emerging deep-sea mining industry. This shift in sourcing has bred the need for new technologies to facilitate the detection and harvest of untapped underwater resources. Belfast-based Descent is one of the pioneer developers of these technologies. The Missive's design challenge was to visually present the scope of Descent's core business. The New York–based design studio had to conduct nearly all of its client interactions long distance via email and phone.

The Process

The Missive team had to do extensive preliminary reading and research on this little known, highly specialized field. Exploration led to dozens of marine- and mining-oriented concept sketches that expanded into a union of ocean waves and mining drills. The application of Eurostile Extended and Bank Gothic Light in the type treatment conveys a visual message of expansion. Screened-back abstract magnifications of coral reef topography and sunken vessels explain where Descent conducts its explorations and tests.

The Result

This eloquent blend of primary and secondary visual messages is instantly recognizable to Descent's core target market. As the industry gains recognition, the logo will surely become instantly recognizable to a broader audience as well—establishing Descent with more than just a leading position in the field.

Screened-back abstract magnifications of coral reef topography and sunken ships on Descent's letterhead explain where the company conducts its explorations and tests.

Descent's minimalist business card design reflects the high-tech nature of its business.

Remix's identity goes where most logo designs fear to tread, employing a number of typefaces to convey a message about data analysis and charting in a nontraditional way.

Hairline rules containing Remix's type treatment communicate the product's ultimate application in charting programs. Easy-to-read icons further illustrate the message on the back of business cards.

Client: **Remix Data**
New York, New York, USA

Agency: **The Missive**
New York, New York

The Challenge
Remix Data is an online retailer that sells raw stock data covering the years 1990 to the present. This data is later imported to a charting program used by investors for analysis and investment decision making. When this division of Nassor Corporation—a software development, management, and consulting firm—wanted a proprietary identity that brought a fresh approach to a staid subject, it called on The Missive. For graphic designers, information and numbers are subjects that pose a true visual challenge, especially when the client asks for a nontraditional solution.

The Process
The Missive's design exploration directed the team toward a type-only approach, concentrating on the analysis of harmonious type relationships. They then focused on selecting a color palette that conveyed the concept of progressive technology without landing on such comfortable islands as gray and blue. The word *Remix* is primarily constructed in Akzidenz Grotesk (with the exception of the distorted Futura plus sign that serves as the letter *X*) and placed on a diagonal perpendicular so the letters *E* and *M* are noticeably and legibly created by the same letterform. The dot-matrix rendering of the word *data* in OCR-B conveys the company's core product. Hairline rules contain the treatment and communicate the product's ultimate application in charting programs.

The Result
Every beginning designer quickly learns that the only place to freely blend fonts is on a ransom note. In this design, however, The Missive demonstrated that successful, original designs can emerge when a designer knows the subtleties of when and how to break important rules.

On its website, Remix's fresh portrayal of statistics and charts conveys a strong point of difference to viewers.

WILDTYPE INFORMATICS
Laboratory Tracking Solutions

*To play up the wild in WildType, Branded Studio distilled a **W** and an I to form a sweeping clawmark that finishes in a concise point—a motion that parallels the company's ability to grab and refine information.*

Client: **WildType Informatics**
San Diego, California, USA

Agency: **Branded Studio, Inc.**
San Diego, California

The Challenge

A software developer of laboratory information management systems, WildType Informatics produces solutions that are in demand in the expanding San Diego biotechnology industry. Its brand—a logo developed in-house before its launch—was already established among its clientele. Now that the company has grown, its founders thought it was time to grow the identity into a professionally produced mark.

The Process

Branded Studio was asked to recreate an icon made from the letters *W* and *I* in the new identity. The team wanted to make more use of the "wild" part of the business's name, which they did by sharpening the points on the *W* and playing with the dimension until a claw was formed. The long wordmark is broken up by diminishing the word *informatics* with the help of screened type. Similarly, the tagline "Laboratory Tracking Solutions" is given secondary placement by means of a screened tint.

The Result

Branded Studio managed to meld *wild* and *precise* into the image by avoiding cliché chaotic portrayals of the concept, opting instead for this subtler animistic approach. Is there anything in nature as wild yet precise as a cat's claw?

While encompassing the parent brand, Senior Publishers Media Group (SPMG), this icon for SPMG's Event Marketing Division contains an abstract but effective message of people gathering around the S.

Client: **Senior Publishers Media Group/Event Marketing Division**
San Diego, California, USA

Agency: **Branded Studio, Inc.**
San Diego, California

The Challenge

According to a recent U.S. census report, every 8.4 seconds, another baby boomer turns 50. Between 1990 and 2020, the elderly population is expected to increase to 54 million. This burgeoning market has more expendable income and buying power than its predecessors. Its ranks are also better educated and read more than any other age group. Senior Publishers Media Group (SMPG) helps products and services reach this powerful target through its network of 300+ grassroots senior publications. Recently, the company extended its range, launching an event marketing division that organizes senior expos filled with product sampling, demonstrations, health seminars and screening as well as one-on-one interaction with sales representatives. This new division needed to establish a point of difference while retaining some elements of its parent identity.

The Process

Branded Studio began its exploration by taking the parent company's original vector file of its logo and ungrouping the elements. They rearranged the pieces until they found that encapsulating the SMPG mark in two large circles and setting a large letter *S* in the background completed the picture.

The Result

The multiple dot elements in the logo are a seemingly minor touch—a bit of background texture. Yet, clustered around the letter *S*, they represent the multitudes of attendees the division is capable of attracting. The Event Marketing Division's identity has already been implemented on video and CD-ROM presentations, CD-ROM packaging, sales book, and a wax stamp. It will eventually be introduced onto its section of the SMPG website and other materials.

Bright, sundrenched photographs used on SPMG's print materials make concrete the company's optimistic mission.

ETHNIC
PRINT • MEDIA • GROUP

Client: **Ethnic Print Media Group**
San Diego, California, USA

Agency: **Branded Studio, Inc.**
San Diego, California

The Challenge

The 35.3 million American Latinos spent $542 billion in 2001 alone. This market segment—representing 13 percent of the nation's total population—has grown 58 percent over the past decade. That's spending power.

A division of Gemstone Productions, Ethnic Print Media Group is the premier Latino print media representative in the United States, offering ROP (run of press/on-page) and FSI (freestanding insert) ad placements in over 200 partner publications. The company planned an expansion of its scope to encompass an additional growth market—African Americans.

The challenge in creating this identity was that it had many messages to send to its target market: the focus on Latino and African American themes and impressions of diversity, growth, ethnicity, and strength.

The Process

Commissioned to develop the identity package, Branded Studio developed dozens of concepts that employed the client's established color palette of warm gold, bronze, tan, cream, and dark brown. An icon depicting the expansion of a single idea into an organic body that changes both shape and color struck a positive chord when presented to the client. A pronounced serif type treatment balanced harmoniously with the weighty icon.

The Result

The client loves the balance and serene power of the new logo, which is now employed on the company's business cards, letterhead, brochures, sales books, reports, website, PowerPoint presentations, custom presentation folders, and trade show display graphics.

Breakthrough.

ROP • FSI
LATINO CO-OP INSERT

Direct your message to the Latino and African American consumer.

ETHNIC
PRINT • MEDIA • GROUP

In their media. In their markets.

p: 866.664.4432 ethnicprintmedia.com

Ethnic Print Media Group's logo communicates both Latino and African American themes while depicting diversity, growth, ethnicity, and strength.

ETHNIC
PRINT • MEDIA • GROUP

TREVOR HANSEN
vice president, sales & marketing

866.664.4432 x203 office
858.272.7275 fax
ethnicprintmedia.com
trevor@ethnicprintmedia.com

¡media que motiva! ™

4901 morena blvd. ste. 203 san diego, ca 92117

Ethnic Print Media Group's icon depicting the expansion of a single idea into an organic body that changes both shape and color strikes a positive chord when paired with English and Spanish text, as seen on this card.

Derived from the Latin word forum—a public gathering place where the judicial process was debated—forensics is the fine art of debate and formal argumentation, which Forensics Institute teaches.

Client: **Forensics Institute, Inc.**
Beverly Hills, California, USA

Agency: **Branded Studio, Inc.**
San Diego, California

The Challenge

Situated in Beverly Hills, the Forensics Institute conducts programs that help legal and political professionals hone their debating skills. To help launch the business, Branded Studio was called in to develop a simple, single-color identity that could be cleanly faxed and printed on a conventional black-and-white printer. In addition to working within these technical limitations, the logo had to convey messages of respect and trust in an abstract concept.

The Process

Exploratory research uncovered the origin of the word *forensics*. Derived from the Latin word *forum*—a public gathering place where the judicial process was debated—forensics is the fine art of debate and formal argumentation. With this information in mind, the Branded Studio team focused on blending an initialism of the company's name with imagery taken from ancient Rome, the birthplace of forensics. Towering, condensed forms of the letters *FII* are transformed into capped and topped columns, creating a stylized image of a forum. A solid foundation of sans serif type supports this intriguing icon.

The Result

Instantly appealing to lawyers and professionals, Forensics Institute's new logo has received great praise from both the client and its customers.

The Forensics Institute initialism is shaped into a symbol of ancient Rome, birthplace of forensics. Towering, condensed forms of the letters FII transform into capped and topped columns, creating a stylized image of a forum on business cards and letterhead.

To entice service industry employees to strive for monetary incentives, Murphy Design created this high-impact, inescapable brand for Aramark's race car–themed initiative.

Client: **The Aramark Corporation/FSS 500**
Philadelphia, Pennsylvania, USA

Agency: **Murphy Design**
Philadelphia, Pennsylvania

The Challenge

The Aramark Corporation is a major player in the services industry, providing large institutions with such diverse services as dining, catering, office coffee, refreshments vending, comprehensive facilities management, childcare and education, uniforms, and safety equipment. The company has many big accounts—government, educational, correctional, sports, and entertainment facilities as well as state parks, national parks, and tourist attractions.

To stimulate growth, the company launched an initiative called FSS 500. Planned around a Formula One racing theme, FSS 500 offered employees across the company an opportunity to earn cash rewards for bringing in new business or additional service business from an existing client.

The Process

Murphy Design researched the graphic themes found at racetracks: the checkerboard flags, the bright contrasting colors of the race cars. The client accepted the concept of a bold graphic portrayal of a race car and driver after viewing it in the context of a proposed newsletter design.

The Result

The FSS 500 mark was branded on mouse pads and individually numbered pit passes as well as three issues of a specialty newsletter. In the end, Aramark was the winner. Its growth initiative goal was not only met but exceeded. Murphy Design's solution was also a winner, garnering a 2002 American Graphic Design Award and a 2003 American Corporate Identity Award.

An arrray of collateral materials, including even a wrist watch, displays the versatility of Aramark's new Formula One–style identity.

WINZO GROUP

Client: **Winzo Group**
Mill Valley, California, USA

Agency: **Project6 Design**
Berkeley, California

The Challenge

Launching new products or repositioning existing brands takes more than deep pockets and a willingness to go out and sell; it takes a dynamic blend of expertise and outside-the-box thinking to reach target audiences and gain market share. Winzo Group is a marketing and strategic positioning company that conducts feasibility studies, analyzes markets, creates collateral materials, and develops new sales channels—all critical components to a successful rollout. Since trend-spotting and professionalism are also a part of the equation, the company needed a dynamic visual presence that spoke these messages loud and clear.

The Process

Commissioned to develop Winzo Group's brand identity, Project6 Design began its exploration with a study of icons that depicted growth, focus, and target. Further research led to the conclusion that a typographic treatment was the only way to express a modern, powerful point of difference. Letterspaced typography, using a contemporary sans serif typeface, was shaped and balanced by the use of a black and red palette that added a touch of sophistication to the overall look.

The Result

The Winzo Group's straight-to-the-point logo dictated the website's clean style and bright, professional palette. The client was thrilled with the solution.

For Winzo, a marketing and strategic positioning company, Project6 created a brand that speaks loud and clear, as customers hope their own brands will under Winzo's care.

WINZO GROUP

Elizabeth Winterhalter

453 Ethel Ave.
Mill Valley, CA 94941
Tel. 415-888-4400
Fax 415-888-4800
elizabeth@winzogroup.com

Winzo Group's icon takes on a subtle dimensionality through the W's shift from center, which adds dynamism to its form.

www.winzogroup.com

SERVICES   CLIENTS   ABOUT WINZO   NEWS   CONTACT US

On its website, Winzo Group continues its dynamic visual presence, speaking messages of trend-right thinking and professionalism.

WINZO GROUP

Launching your product or service is the most critical investment your company makes.

Reaching target markets effectively and building early sales momentum takes more than a good idea. Successful rollouts require careful strategic planning, dedicated resources and flawless execution.

Winzo Group is an established marketing firm that specializes in product launch and positioning. We provide a full range of services – from developing new sales channels and supporting collateral material to competitive positioning and analysis – all designed to increase your market share.

Strategic and Tactical Direction in Product Launch and Repositioning. Providing Market Leadership

Anodyne

Andoyne's refreshed identity addresses its state-of-the-art and current positioning as a trusted resource and leading supplier of biomedical equipment—an equity built over 20 years.

Client: **Anodyne**
Minnetonka, Minnesota, USA

Agency: **Franke + Fiorella**
Minneapolis, Minnesota

The Challenge

A distributor of medical supplies for more than 20 years, Anodyne wanted to refresh its identity and visually position itself in a new light to its healthcare audience—as a trusted resource for biomedical equipment such as cryotherapy and transcutaneous electrical nerve stimulation devices. The firm's visual identity had to be as state of the art and current as the products it sells to the medical community.

The Process

The Franke + Fiorella design team conducted a competitive audit to uncover the need for a mark that conveyed reliability and confidence and commanded respect while appearing unique amid the sea of brochures and business cards that crowd most hospital managers' desks. The design exploration phase led to the development of a classic serif type treatment that incorporated a medical cross in the center of the letter *o*. Green, often used to signify health, became the predominant palette color for the identity. As an added touch, a magnified shadow of the logo is employed to convey dynamism and action.

The Result

Anodyne's success and growth in the medical community speaks to the work Franke + Fiorella did refreshing the brand.

A medical cross in the center of the letter o, green color palette, and magnified shadowing of its name communicate Anodyne's messages of dynamism, action, and health.

FREE␣OTION™

Balance, strength, and stability are the core messages conveyed in FreeMotion Fitness's cutting-edge identity: messages that have successfully resonated with the USA Tennis High Performance Program Center and the YMCA, who have designated the company an official provider.

Client: **FreeMotion Fitness**
Colorado Springs, Colorado, USA

Agency: **Hornall Anderson Design Works, Inc.**
Seattle, Washington, USA

The Challenge

The fitness equipment industry has grown by leaps and bounds over the past 30 years, encompassing the health club, physical therapy, spa, and at-home fitness consumer markets. The commercial division of ICON Health and Fitness, FreeMotion, is a leading provider of strength and cardio fitness equipment for this huge segment. The Hornall Anderson Design Works (HADW) team was faced with a particularly daunting challenge when FreeMotion first contacted them after the tragedy of 9/11. The fitness equipment manufacturer had been called Ground Zero, but after the terrorist attacks on the World Trade Center in New York City—a site that came to be called Ground Zero—the Colorado company determined it was prudent to change its name.

The Process

The HADW design team initiated the process by conducting an intensive name study. This effort included focus group research and position development to ensure the new identity would reflect the company's state-of-the-art equipment and training philosophy: to create cutting-edge equipment that helps people build core strength, balance, and stability.

The Result

Since the launch of its new identity, FreeMotion has been designated the official training equipment of the USA Tennis High-Performance Program Center and the YMCA.

The result of an intensive name search that took place after the tragedy of 9/11, FreeMotion's identity addresses the company's strength plus cardio fitness training philosophy and the state-of-the-art nature of its equipment in its logo, color scheme, and supporting imagery.

AUTODESTRUCT SYRINGE TECHNOLOGY

Client: **K1 Syringe**
East Sussex, UK

Agency: **Lewis Moberly**
London, UK

The Challenge

Medical supplies, and especially syringes, are difficult to brand with expressions of user friendliness and safety. It's also tough to stand out in an extremely crowded marketplace where every product launch makes the same promises. Created by Star Syringe Ltd., K1 is an auto-destruct syringe with an ingenious yet simple device that renders the syringe nonfunctional after one injection. This point of difference is strong; its construction makes it impossible to use the unit again, eliminating the potential spread of disease. Lewis Moberly was charged with designing a brand identity to stand out among numerous competitors, an identity that would underscore the core concept and highlight the product's additional messages: that the syringe can be used with confidence and is produced inexpensively enough to market in developing nations, where low-cost medical supplies are desperately needed. Consequently, the brand's logo had to be highly legible and able to read across numerous languages and literacy levels.

The Process

The Lewis Moberly design team created an identity that required no secondary messages or translation—a syringe shape formed within the type treatment. The mark is so distinctive it makes a strong impression even when printed on the barrel of the smallest unit.

The Result

Besides clearly delivering the message, K1 and its visual identity team have received a greater reward—knowing they've had a positive impact on world health. The Chinese government estimates 20,000 lives have been saved by this low-cost medical device since it was introduced. Furthermore, Lewis Moberly received a Millennium Product Award and won the DBA Design Effectiveness Judges' Special Award for the solution.

Messages of user friendliness and safety coupled with the need for a strong visual point of difference in an extremely crowded marketplace were only minor challenges posed in the design of the K1 syringe logo. The real test came in the identity's ability to read across numerous languages and literacy levels.

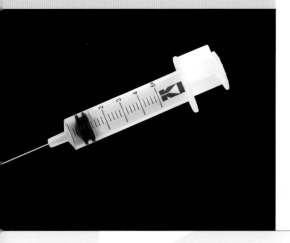

A syringe shape formed within K1's type treatment yields an image so distinctive it makes a strong impression even when printed on the barrel of the smallest unit.

K1's dynamic logo serves as the basis for striking support imagery used in its collateral program, which won Lewis Moberly a Millennium Product Award and a DBA Design Effectiveness Judges' Special Award.

AUTODESTRUCT FOR IMMUNIZATION

Disposable syringes **should only be used once.** K1 syringes **can only be used once.**

There is nothing complicated about K1 syringes; they are used in the standard way and are suitable in any situation.

Using K1 syringes is the responsible way to reduce the spread of disease.

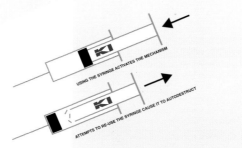

USING THE SYRINGE ACTIVATES THE MECHANISM

ATTEMPTS TO RE-USE THE SYRINGE CAUSE IT TO AUTODESTRUCT

There is no need for user re-education. K1 syringes look the same as standard ones, fill only to 0.5ml, and after an injection has been given, it automatically destroys itself.

K1 TECHNOLOGY – THE NEXT GENERATION OF SYRINGES

Medco Health's bright identity speaks of the company's humanness, care, and promise of health, employing a green and sunshine-orange palette and accessible type treatment.

Client: **Medco Health**

Franklin Lakes, New Jersey, USA

Agency: **Lippincott Mercer**

New York, New York, USA

The Challenge

Medco Health is the nation's leading pharmacy benefits manager, delivering 537 million prescriptions to more than 62 million people in 2002. That represents nearly one in four Americans. The company provides prescription services for 190 Fortune 500 companies, 12 of the nation's 42 Blue Cross/Blue Shield plans, and several large managed care organizations. In addition, Medco's Systemed LLC capitalizes on its extensive PBM (pharmacy benefit management) capabilities to meet the specific needs of small- to mid-sized clients. Medco Health's educational programs and sophisticated information systems link patients, pharmacists, and physicians, helping ensure the appropriate use of prescription drugs for each individual based on individual health profile, best clinical practices, and benefit plan coverage. Lippincott Mercer was charged with developing a visual brand that portrayed Medco Health's ability to help control total healthcare costs, improve quality of care, and provide member satisfaction.

The Process

Lippincott Mercer and Medco Health embarked on a collaborative creative process. Together, client and agency developed a wide range of design solutions that included logotypes, wordmarks, and symbols. Each potential concept was tested against positioning and image attributes during intensive research. The final image combines symbols of health—sunshine and a sprouting leaf—with a positive orange and green palette.

The Result

Lippincott Mercer's solution was widely embraced within the Medco Health organization. The design team worked closely with the client to develop identity standards to effectively and efficiently manage implementation of the new brand identity, which appears on stationery, collateral materials, and its website.

Medco Health's promise of health is conveyed through its sun and leaf icon. In collateral materials and on a website, the theme continues in the incorporation of lively photographs of the people the organization serves.

Lippincott Mercer worked closely with the client to develop identity standards to effectively and efficiently manage implementation of the new brand identity.

PRECISION LASER HAIR REMOVAL

A nongender-specific depiction of hair strands and a neutral palette attract both men and women to New York Gynecology and Obstetrician Association's Exfolica laser hair removal and spa treatment services.

Using an attractive man and woman to convey the promise of model-quality beauty on collateral materials, ads, and website pages, Exfolica maintained the loyalty of its female customer base while attracting new male clientele.

Client: **New York Gynecology and Obstetrician Association (NYGOA)**
New York, New York, USA

Agency: **Outside the Box Interactive LLC**
New York, New York

The Challenge

New York Gynecology and Obstetrician Association (NYGOA) is one of New York City's leading medical groups. To leverage consumer demand for safe, medically supervised cosmetic beauty treatments, the organization decided to add laser hair removal—called epilation—to its roster. The Outside the Box Interactive design team confronted a number of challenges when commissioned to develop an identity for the new service. Usually associated with dermatological treatment, the new service didn't quite fit NYGOA's recognized scope of practice. The medical group's perceived expertise and quality of service had to be conveyed in the new brand. Finally, the identity had to attract men as well as NYGOA's established female clientele.

The Process

The Out of the Box Interactive team researched, culled, and vetted over 50 potential names for the new service. Through focus groups, studies, and narrowing their defined objectives, the team refined the search to two distinct directions. One leveraged the procedure's guarantee of safety through medical supervision. The other spoke to consumers' perceived association between laser hair removal and spa treatments, using an attractive man and woman to convey the promise of model-quality beauty.

The Result

The Out of the Box Interactive team developed a complete communications program to launch the new NYGOA offering. Applications include a brochure, counter card, statement stuffer, miniwebsite, and stationery system. It has been employed in cross promotions with health clubs, upscale hotels, and spas. The identity program also included a DVD presentation that was displayed on a monitor in the facility's waiting room and mailed to a list of existing clients and to prospects harvested from purchased mailing lists. A full-scale website, launched later in the program, features online scheduling and a streaming version of the DVD presentation.

GlaxoSmithKline's new logo leverages the equity of two pharmaceutical giants while establishing a new brand in the eyes of consumers and medical professionals.

Client: **GlaxoSmithKline**
Research Triangle Park, North Carolina, USA

Agency: **FutureBrand**
New York, New York, USA

The Challenge

When two pharmaceutical giants merged to become GlaxoSmithKline (GSK), the newly formed entity needed a new vision, a new brand, and a new corporate identity that would appeal to both consumer and medical audiences without jeopardizing the success of existing product brands. The new company contracted FutureBrand to create an open and approachable identity that would maintain a balance between a strong corporate brand and the individual character of the company's divisions—one that would resonate with a diverse audience. GSK's new identity had to build awareness, strengthen consumer loyalty, inspire employees, and lead organizational change—all in record time.

The Process

The FutureBrand team first identified changes in the pharmaceutical industry, such as the growing importance of consumer marketing, the emergence of patients as consumers, and the proliferation of consumer information. The team worked with GSK to develop a positioning platform that embraced a strong mission: "to improve the quality of human life by enabling people to do more, feel better, and live longer."

GSK needed to appear to be more than a monolithic corporation. FutureBrand's design studies centered on the emotional aspects of wellness. The final image is an abstract silhouette of a human heart. The team executed the image in a warm, healthy orange palette that symbolizes vitality and hope.

The Result

To implement the new identity, FutureBrand developed a proprietary online system that manages all of the brand assets with one coordinated global tool. One of the greatest successes of the program was helping merge the cultures of the two organizations. The brand was used as a catalyst for the merger as well as a symbol of the combined ethos and mission of this new institution. Reactions from senior management included comments such as, "It's fantastic. This company looks and feels different," and "I feel like we've had this logo forever."

An abstract silhouette of a human heart, executed in a warm, healthy orange palette that symbolizes vitality and hope, encompasses an initialism of the company's name. Used on brochures, CD-ROM presentations, and even mouse pads, the new image not only resonated well with target audiences but also helped merge the cultures of the two organizations.

*A pair of glasses replaces
the letter B in Buona Vista's
name, which literally means
"good vision." The logo
comes in three versions:
a gold foil rendition for
packaging, a two-color
version for print work, and
a one-color version for
shipping materials.*

Client: **Diva International/Buona Vista**
Spello, Italy

Agency: **Studio GT&P**
Foligno, Italy

The Challenge

The majority of world's products are developed to appeal to either male or female consumers. Once the gender market is determined, other marketing factors are incorporated into the equation. Packaging and message points are directed to appeal to specific demographic and economic segments as well as sophistication-level and age-related subgroups derived from focus group sessions, supply and demand studies, and trend analysis. Through this intensive process, marketers develop a personality profile of the product's ideal customer. Men and women of all ages use lens cleaning papers to maintain sunglasses, prescription and over-the-counter eyewear, even camera equipment. The market is saturated with products that target a general audience. To create a point of difference in this arena, Diva International set out to launch Buona Vista—lens cleaning papers targeted to an upscale female audience.

The Process

The Studio GT&P design team focused on portraying the product's intended use in the identity's typographic treatment. A pair of glasses replaces the letter *B* in the company's name, which literally means "good vision." Applied in gold foil on packaging and on displays, the logo was also designed in a two-color version and a black version for use in other materials.

The Result

The client was impressed with the result. Thus far, Studio GT&P's brand identity for the recently launched Buona Vista lens cleaning papers has been applied to packaging, displays, and collateral materials.

*Narrowly targeting an
upscale female audience,
Buona Vista lens cleaning
papers create a point of difference in a saturated market that normally targets a
general audience.*

InvoCare

Innovation, vocation, and caring are the positive messages portrayed in this identity for Australia's largest provider of funerary services.

Client: **SCIA**
Sydney, Australia

Agency: **Cato Purnell Partners**
Richmond, Australia

The Challenge

The funeral business is changing as people's attitudes about death and dying evolve. There is more open dialog among businesses that service the industry and consumers than ever before. There is also more caring and compassion on both sides. In 2003, Australia's largest provider of funerary services, SCIA, restructured and rebranded itself to maintain its position as an industry leader. The name InvoCare was developed for SCIA to reflect its corporate positioning of innovation, vocation, and caring. True to the new name, InvoCare has been active in the communities it serves, working with charitable organizations such as Save the Children, Grief Support, and Rotary.

The Process

The Cato Purnell design team was assigned the job of creating an image that would narrate InvoCare's messages in a positive way. Numerous sketches led to the development of an icon that represents the nurturing and all-encompassing approach the company takes in dealing with is clients and the community. A sense of commitment and dedication are conveyed through the brand's bold, classic, serif type treatment. These elements were combined with a serene, positive palette of warm gray and lavender that speaks of the company's innovative approach to an otherwise dark, somber subject.

The Result

Cato Purnell's new InvoCare identity reveals a new abstract form for the concept of caring and comforting, which has so often been associated with a hand or hands. Here, a broken circle enveloped by a complete circle gives new shape to a fundamental idea. The client quickly approved the new mark and implemented it in its stationery program, collateral materials, and website.

The brand identity for ProBeauty Beauty and Cosmetic Surgery takes a gentle, sensitive approach to its subject, using a subdued color palette and emotional imagery to communicate the beauty, self-confidence, and peace of mind that can be achieved through cosmetic surgery.

Das medizinische Laser- und Kosmetikzentrum

pro*beauty*

The gentle, sensitive approach to ProBeauty's identity is also implemented in the clinic's reception area. The approach has been so successful that a second clinic is being launched along Germany's northern coast.

Client: **ProBeauty Beauty and Cosmetic Surgery**
Bremerhaven, Germany

Agency: **Braue: Branding & Corporate Design**
Bremerhaven, Germany

The Challenge

As the industrialized nations' population ages, the majority of senior consumers seek more and better ways to maintain their youthful appearance and improve their looks. Medical science and beauty companies have teamed up with science and technology to develop ways whereby consumers can transform sagging jawlines and angled noses. ProBeauty and Cosmetic Surgery offers these services within a caring and medically safe environment. Braue: Branding & Corporate Design was called in to develop a visual identity that would convey that message while also communicating the trust and confidence consumers demand.

The Process

Braue's design team thoroughly explored this subject by trend scouting, researching the cosmetic surgery industry, conducting extensive target audience interviews, and reading special interest magazines. With data in hand, the team set its limits: Keep consumers from thinking about scalpels, tubes, and scars. They took a gentle, sensitive approach by employing a subdued color palette and emotional imagery to communicate the beauty, self-confidence, and peace of mind that can be achieved through cosmetic surgery.

The Result

How do you make a client smile? Help boost their bottom line. Since this logo was implemented on ProBeauty's signage, stationery program, brochures, presentation folders, posters, website, and advertising campaign, the clinic has experienced strong growth culminating in the opening of a second clinic on Germany's northern coast.

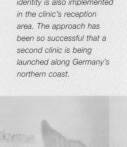

To keep consumers from associating cosmetic surgery with scalpels, tubes, and scars, a butterfly is employed as a reminder of the beauty that emerges as a result of the organization's services.

Murphy Design's last-minute, one-color identity for a trade show display proved to be the straightforward solution Aramark was seeking.

Client: **The Aramark Corporation/Mission One Medical Center**
Philadelphia, Pennsylvania, USA

Agency: **Murphy Design**
Philadelphia, Pennsylvania

The Challenge
A leader in institutional food service and facility management, the Aramark Corporation provides myriad services to businesses, government, educational, correctional, and health care facilities as well as sports, entertainment, and convention centers, plus national parks and tourist attractions.

To increase its market share in the ever-growing health care arena, Aramark created a trade show display targeted at the nation's hospital and healthcare facilities. Mission One Medical Center is a virtual hospital that demonstrates the many ways Aramark can improve operations in a hospital setting. Murphy Design was called in at the last minute to create a one-color typographic logo for this one-time event.

The Process
Considering the crunch deadline, the designer team chose a straightforward solution that used *M1* as an icon. A letterspaced serif type treatment provided the mark with a reliable and respectable presence. Variations on this core concept were emailed as PDF files to Aramark's four-person review panel for final selection.

The Result
When the final design was approved, the Mission One Medical Center mark was applied to signage, presentation folders, and other support materials just in time for its one-time-only display. Though the duration of this brand was too brief to measure its impact conventionally, the fact that the client quickly returned to Murphy with additional work sums up Aramark's opinion of the logo.

Intensive Care Unit: Reducing Barriers for Care Providers

- Dependable clinical equipment

- Rapid bed turnaround to ease capacity constraints

- Timely transportation of patients and supplies

Informational placards created for the trade show demonstrate the designer's intuitive use of one color in a type treatment.

A strong visual message of joints in motion is enhanced by the reference to the product's name—CSC-II—in this identity for a natural collagen-replacement product that promotes joint health and improves mobility.

Client: **Wheatland Naturals/CSC II**
Shattuck, Oklahoma, USA

Agency: **CFX Creative**
Vancouver, British Columbia, Canada

The Challenge

Preventive health care is a crucial message in the field of alternative remedies. As a large portion of the consumer market is over age 40, natural remedy manufacturers have set their sights on supplying consumers with products that can mitigate the effects of aging, from weakened memory to joint pain. Wheatland Naturals, a pioneer in this field, developed a collagen-replacement product called CSC-II (chicken sternum collagen type II) that promotes joint health and improves mobility. CFX Creative was asked to develop a brand for the product that would possess a strong visual point of difference.

The Process

A competitive audit of store shelves led to the conclusion that a bold iconic treatment coupled with clean, legible typography was the answer. Exploring rounded shapes and letterforms, the team developed a shape that united the letters *CC* in the center, creating an abstract *S*. The strong visual message of joints in motion is enhanced by the reference to the product's name: CSC.

The Result

At the time of writing, it's still too early to know what the effect will be, but the client embraced the logo and will be launching under the CSC-II mark distinctive identity in 2004. The brand will appear on the product's retail packaging, labeling, and sell sheets.

Contextualized on the product's container, the logo is complemented by a courteous sans serif type treatment.

Client: **MedBiz Market**
Baton Rouge, Louisiana, USA

*MedBiz Market's logo
focuses on the interaction
between buyer and seller
within a health care–oriented
real estate marketplace. By
incorporating a hard-edged
business font and colors
commonly found in hospitals,
the designers were able to
address both markets.*

Agency: **CFX Creative**
Vancouver, British Columbia, Canada

The Challenge

MedBiz Market has over 30 years of experience in the healthcare industry, ranging from facility development to daily operations management. The company extended its scope to offer prospective buyers and sellers an online resource for the sale of medical offices, pharmacies, hospitals, medical supply houses, nursing homes, assisted living residences, and other health care facilities. It assists buyers in securing financing for purchases.

CFX Creative was given the task of developing a brand identity that would portray both the medical and business aspects of the company's offering. Because the mark would predominantly be employed on the Web, it had to have a clean and easily recognizable presence.

*The new logo's color palette,
as well as the designer's
solid typography system, is
continued throughout
MedBiz's website.*

The Process

Rather than spelling out a message of real estate, the CFX Creative design team directed its attention to the interaction between buyer and seller within the marketplace. Pairs of gray and green arrows pointing in four directions graphically achieved the goal. The icon was combined with a solid, sans serif type treatment that gives equal weight to both the medical and business sides of the company's wordmark. The color green is traditionally associated with the medical profession, making it the perfect palette to convey the identity to the target market.

The Result

Initially, the identity was implemented on MedBiz Market's eponymously named website, accompanied by the tagline "The Marketplace for Healthcare Buyers and Sellers." The client was so pleased with viewer response it plans to incorporate the mark into a full corporate identity package.

díva

Client: **Diva International Srl**
Spello, Italy

Agency: **Studio GT&P**
Foligno, Italy

The Challenge

Health care products and services developed for use strictly by women has become a flourishing industry. From prescription and over-the-counter medications to natural and alternative remedies, the women's health industry demands a design treatment that conveys messages of confidence, trust, reliability, and femininity, all in one image.

Diva International creates lines of products that target this huge audience of women. Studio GT&P was asked to create a vital yet feminine identity combining warmth, softness, energy, and strength in a single image.

The Process

Studio GT&P's solution to the challenge of designing packaging for Diva International's line of products focused on the use of the structurally perfect typeface Bodoni in a modified form. A blue color palette enhances the sense of reliability the image needed. A golden brushstroke reflects the human aspect of well-being and healthcare that is a signature of Diva International's product line.

The Result

The brand was instantly accepted by its target audience, and the client loves it. It appears on all of their branded products and on signage, collateral materials, and the company's stationery program.

Confidence, trust, reliability, and, above all, femininity are the messages conveyed in Diva International's blue and gold identity.

Offering beauty and health care products for an upscale female audience, Diva International combines the human touch, warmth, softness, energy, and strength in its brand identity.

Diva's proprietary line of beauty and health aids, such as this box of single-use makeup remover and cleansing towelettes, has an elegant, distinctive air that appeals to its target market.

Presented in both Mandarin characters and Roman letters, Sen's name and image fuse two cultures to send the company's message of "living balance" to consumers. Sen is the Mandarin word for "forest," a universal symbol of an ideal ecosystem that's continually evolving yet constantly in balance.

Client: **Sen**
            London, UK

Agency: **Wolff Olins**
            London, UK

The Challenge

Hutchison Whampoa is one of the largest companies listed on the Hong Kong stock exchange, with more than 150,000 staff in businesses spanning 41 countries. This massive conglomerate decided to bring good quality, reliable, and well-packaged traditional Chinese medicine products to the West. For most Westerners, Chinese medicine is an unknown entity. Potential consumers are concerned about product content. Generally speaking, this target audience lacks understanding and is sometimes skeptical of the effectiveness of these ancient formulas. Wolff Olins was commissioned to create not only the brand but the business strategy for Hutchison Whampoa's latest enterprise.

The biggest task for the Wolff Olins creative team was to demystify perceptions of Chinese medicine and to create a brand that would attract customers to this ancient healing art and help them feel comfortable with it. The new identity had to retain its Chinese heritage and resonate with the West. The name had to be meaningful in the Chinese language, but English-speaking consumers had to be able to pronounce it.

The Process

The Wolff Olins team began its investigations by discovering what products would be sold outside of China. The team visited the two Chinese production factories and researched how the products were marketed and used within China. The team also did extensive research into the alternative therapies industry and its target audiences.

Chinese medicine seeks to achieve balance between the body and the natural world. These two elements provided the creative team with the brand's essence: "living balance." This concept catapulted them toward the Mandarin word for "forest," which is *sen*. In both Eastern and Western cultures, the forest represents an ideal ecosystem that is continually evolving yet constantly in balance. The Chinese character for the word *sen* is made up of three smaller "wood" characters arranged in a triangular formation, creating a beautiful and visually memorable identity.

The Result

Hutchison Whampoa launched its Sen product line in central London with the opening of the first Sen shop in December 2003. Since then, Sen concessions have been launched in British pharmacies such as Boots and Lloyds. While it's still in its early days, the Sen designs were recognized in 2003 by the London International Advertising and Design Awards and the prestigious British Design and Advertising Awards.

The Chinese character for the word sen is made up of three smaller "wood" characters arranged in a triangular formation, creating a beautiful and visually memorable identity in both packaging and store signage.

The identity's bright palette continues the theme of positive energy, health, and quality even on its website, which supports the product line's launch in chain pharmacies throughout the United Kingdom.

health

Traditional Chinese Medicine treats illnesses holistically - it looks at root causes not surface problems.

Often 'illnesses' referred to in Western medicine would actually be considered as symptoms in tcm - possibly caused by body network weakness that the West would not expect to be connected.

To see how tcm views some common symptoms (or illnesses), select one of the following:

[cold or flu ⬍] [GO]

S**I**MON'S
ESPRESSO CAFE

To show that Simon of Simon's Espresso Café is an actual person, Daigle Design used a symbolic male figure for the I in Simon.

Client: **Simon's Espresso Café**
Seattle, Washington, USA

Agency: **Daigle Design**
Bainbridge Island, Washington

The Challenge

It takes more than a great latte to attract the attention of coffee consumers in Seattle, where cafés and coffee shops are as numerous as newsstands in New York. Simon's Espresso Café needed a visual point of difference to make its way in this highly-competitive marketplace. Daigle Design was called in to create that identity.

The Process

The designers wanted to establish recognition of Simon as a person, so they incorporated the figure of a man into the logo's typographic treatment. Numerous sketches and fonts were reviewed to find the perfect downtown-Seattle, metropolitan café feel. The man-shaped *I* was enhanced by a provocative shadow, which was tried at many angles before final selection was made. The *I* was later employed as a motif on takeout cups and other materials.

The Result

The logo, which is currently used in packaging, cups, signage, and collateral materials in the highly competitive coffee arena in Seattle, received a 2003 national design award from American Corporate Identity.

The logo's iconic I stands alone on cups and other printed materials and, in repetition, makes a strong motif.

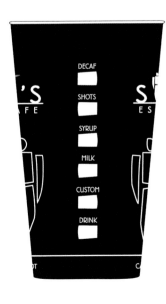

*Young sprouting leaves,
an elegant cursive font,
and subtle gold trim speak
of spring to Spring Park
International Hotels'
Asian market.*

Client: **Spring Park International Hotels**
               Taipei, Taiwan

Agency: **Graphicwise**
               Irvine, California, USA

The Challenge

Based in Taiwan, Spring Park International Hotels' owner wanted a high-end logo for the exclusive chain of Far Eastern hotels. He also wanted the word *spring* to be symbolized in the finished visual identity. The biggest challenge Graphicwise faced when it was commissioned to develop the logo was time; the client didn't contact the design team until the hotels were a month from opening.

The Process

Following the strict request to symbolize spring in the design solution, the Graphicwise team went through numerous intensive brainstorms, emerging with two potential symbols—a butterfly and young sprouting leaves. The latter was selected because it was more strongly connected to the season's association with birth and growth. The cursive font added a touch of elegance that resonated well with the hotel chain's Asian locales and audience. The team also recommended parts of the leaf motif be stamped with a subtle shade of gold foil.

The Result

Graphicwise's final design was unveiled before the Taiwanese press when the hotels were just about to open for business. The logo was applied to everything from the stationery program, robes, towels, and bed covers to hotel signage, website, print advertising, and billboards. It earned Graphicwise a 2002 American Design Awards gold award.

春秋國際股份有限公司

春秋國際股份有限公司
電話: +886-2-2775-5877 傳真: +886-2-2775-5261
地址: 106台北市延吉街162號3樓之一
網址: www.springparkhotel.com.tw

Spring Park International Co., Ltd.
Tel: +886-2-2775-5877 Fax: +886-2-2775-5261
Address: 3F-1, No. 162 Yen-Chi Street, Taipei, Taiwan 106, R.O.C.
www.springparkhotel.com.tw

Edwin Chang
Chairman

Tel: +886-2-2775-5877
Fax: +886-2-2775-5261
Email: chm@springparkhotel.com.tw
Web Site: www.springparkhotel.com.tw
Address: 3F-1, No. 162 Yen-Chi Street, Taipei, Taiwan 106, R.O.C.

Screened-back enlargements of the young leaves icon, seen here on business cards and letterhead, reinforces the branding.

The Lewis Moberly design team created this informal script type treatment which was inspired by the whimsical drawing style found in many Italian village cafés and patisseries.

Lewis Moberly didn't stop with the logo: they created an extensive series of playful graphic illustrations used to extend the branding on printed materials, packaging, and signage.

Client: **Panini/Grand Hyatt Hotel Dubai**
Dubai, United Arab Emirates

Agency: **Lewis Moberly**
London, UK

The Challenge

The Grand Hyatt Dubai Hotel is one of the Middle East's largest and most exclusive hotels, appealing to both business and leisure travelers. The establishment houses 674 rooms and suites as well as 15 restaurants and bars, each with a distinct personality.

The Grand Hyatt's bakery café and patisserie, Panini, is designed in the style of a classic Italian village café. Panini's identity had to communicate a sophisticated version of this persona as well as advertise the venue's offerings: delicate pastries, cakes, chocolates, gelati, and gift packaging. To accomplish this goal, the hotel hired Lewis Moberly, which had previously developed the brand for another of the Grand Hyatt's venues, Indochine (see page 98).

The Process

The Lewis Moberly design team took its inspiration from the whimsical drawing style found in many Italian village cafés and patisseries. The informal script type treatment and spontaneous graphic illustration are set on a bold red. The team's solution plays on the lively, fun, relaxed, and social elements that can be found at these establishments, which serve as the lifeblood of small towns throughout Italy.

The Result

Panini's lighthearted logo playfully decorates the café's menus and signage as well as numerous takeout items. The cafe was an immediate success with hotel visitors, who find the expressive branding an open invitation to take a pampering break. Lewis Moberly won accolades for its solution, including designations from Creativity 33 Annual and Mobius 2003.

Lewis Moberly designed this expressive logo for Vinopolis to emphasize wine passion and eschew snobbery.

Logo details on packaging and signage further the brand's message of accessible, sensual enjoyment.

VINOPOLIS
CITY OF WINE

Vinopolis, a new wine destination on the banks of the River Thames, houses 20 walk-through rooms, where visitors can taste wines, learn about viniculture, and purchase wines and wine accoutrements. Plus, there is a restaurant offering more wines by the glass than any other in Europe.

Client: **Wineworld plc**
London, UK

Agency: **Lewis Moberly**
London, UK

The Challenge

Vinopolis is visitor attraction on a grand scale. A major new venture on the banks of the River Thames, the venue presents a rare opportunity to experience and learn about wine in depth, covering every conceivable aspect from grape to glass. The complex consists of 20 halls. Each hall hosts a particular region, presenting a visual feast that narrates the host's wine-related history, culture, and character. Audio commentary is provided by the world's leading wine experts. Grand Tasting Halls, a shop, a gallery, and a restaurant offering more wines by the glass than any other in Europe complete the experience.

Lewis Moberly was commissioned to create a brand that broke down the wine snobbery barriers, emotionally and visually captivating audiences who want to learn more about wine and wine appreciation. The design solution also had to attract investors needed to acquire the £18 million in funding for completion.

The Process

Wine affects more than one sense. In fact, the true appreciation of wine involves sight, smell, taste, and touch. The Lewis Moberly creative team focused on these essentials of wine appreciation to create a compelling visual invitation to this distinctive London destination. The design solution was an abstract view of the human senses paired with the true wine experience, creating an inviting and intriguing statement. Applying a Picasso-style motif to the overall treatment, the identity resonates with both veteran aficionados and novices who equate wine with fine art.

The Result

Working closely with interior design house Jasper Jacobs Associates, Lewis Moberly employed the identity in collateral and promotional materials, signage, and shopping bags. The complete visual package not only attracts thousands of visitors, it won the agency a number of awards, including a Loewrie Gold Award, the D&AD Annual, and a Clio Bronze.

LA GRAN**DE**
EPICERIE **PARIS**

The Lewis Moberly team experimented extensively with word pairings until they identified this deceptively simple solution, which reduces a long name to a strong logotype.

Client: **Le Bon Marché**
Paris, France

Agency: **Lewis Moberly**
London, UK

The Challenge

La Grande Epicerie de Paris, situated in Paris's stately Le Bon Marché department store, is the city's leading food hall. A longstanding institution on the Rive Gauche, the store's food department offers an international array of over 5,000 products, from hard-to-find Welsh mineral water and handmade French jams to piquant Neopolitan tomato sauce and organic provincial sausages. Lewis Moberly was commissioned to create a fresh, new identity that targets new "foodies" and clearly demonstrates the contemporary and confident stance of La Grande Epicerie de Paris. The challenge was to convey a long name on a range of materials—from entry signage to the top of a delicately iced pastry.

The Process

The Lewis Moberly design team carefully scrutinized the food hall's name, observing the relationship of the words and their meaning within the store, on signage, packaging, and all other printed materials. Intensive experimentation with fonts led to a deceptively simple and modern typographic solution. Further crafting with fonts and layout led to the final design, in which shared letterforms make the most of a long name and emphasize the food store's longstanding importance to life on the Rive Gauche.

The City of Lights' leading food hall and a venerable institution on the Rive Gauche, La Grande Epicerie de Paris's image evoked its belle epoque roots, but said little about its contemporary and international array of foods.

Emblazoned on the storefront, the optical illusion is so smooth that it reads instantly as the full name. The font choice emphasizes contemporary products and high quality.

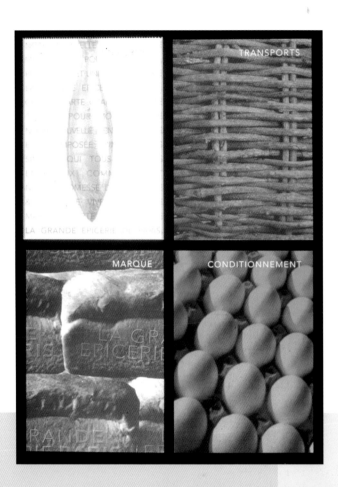

The Result

The logo and overall identity were implemented across the entire retail environment from signage and uniforms to cake boxes and van liveries. The store's diverse range of customers immediately accepted the refreshed identity; now patrons, both young and old, proudly promenade through the Parisian streets with La Grande Epicerie de Paris shopping bags. The design has received numerous awards, including designations from British Design and Art Direction, Mobius Advertising Awards, and the Loerie Awards.

While the clean white packaging assures food customers of purity and cleanliness, the signage expresses a photographic and illustrative romance with food.

Client: **Indochine/Grand Hyatt Hotel Dubai**
Dubai, United Arab Emirates

Agency: **Lewis Moberly**
London, UK

The Challenge

Indochine is a Vietnamese family-style noodle restaurant, one of 15 bars and eating establishments housed at the luxury hotel Grand Hyatt Dubai. Bringing the delicate flavors of Vietnam to Dubai for the first time, Indochine focuses on authenticity in its décor and cuisine. The venue has an airy, elegant, yet contemporary interior featuring light woods, beaten metal, and a striking calligraphy-adorned ceiling. Its chefs were recruited from Vietnam's finest restaurants. The Vietnamese waitstaff is well versed in the cuisine, able to explain the intricate orchestration of ingredients and preparation techniques to diners. The Lewis Moberly design team was contracted to create Indochine's identity, which had to reflect the depth and richness of this southeast Asian culture.

The Process

The Lewis Moberly team presented several concepts to the client, the most charming of which that won the day. After careful research into Vietnamese culture as well as Southeast Asian symbols and motifs, the team developed an identity that employs a sophisticated color palette and textures that pay homage to Thai wood engravings. In contrast, the identity's central image focuses on three pairs of playful Indo-Chinese characters playing a noodle-puzzle game.

The Result

The logo's bold illustration style supports readability and definition both at a small size and when engraved or printed on wood veneers and silks as part of the interior design. Indochine's finished identity and ambient restaurant interior transports the diner instantly into a new world. From signage and menus to cuisine and atmosphere, the entire brand identity communicates the Vietnamese experience.

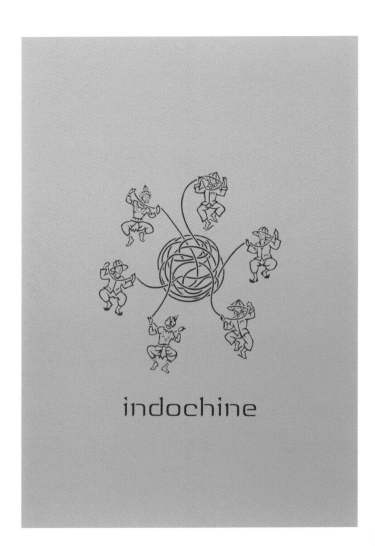

To introduce Dubai's first Vietnamese restaurant, Lewis Moberly drew on Vietnamese and Thai influences as well as the restaurant's color scheme. The logo portrays three pairs of people engaged in a noodle-puzzle game.

The signage has been remarkably effective. It has even drawn business away from the nearby Starbucks.

Client: **Bellatazza**
Bend, Oregon, USA

Agency: **Panagrafik**
Bend, Oregon

The Challenge

Many clients, whether large or small, don't have a specific vision in mind when they ask for a logo design, so it's easy to direct them down a logical, tasteful path. Bellatazza was quite different in this respect. The owners had a strong vision of what they wanted when they asked Paragrafik to create a brand identity for this Oregon Italian coffee shop.

The Process

Perfection was the driving force in this project from beginning to end. All aspects of the identity's hand-lettered type treatment had to be perfect: the letterforms, the slant, the spacing. About 300 versions were executed with a high-quality sable watercolor brush and India ink.

The Result

Implemented on signage, packaging, promotional items, and advertising, Bellatazza's visual identity has pulled in a large market share of the local café business. The café has enticed office and retail employees who work right next door to a Starbucks to walk a block up the street for their daily caffeine fix.

The Panagrafik team hand painted over 300 versions of Bellatazza's logo with a sable brush to obtain perfect strokes. The accompanying icon is used to create patterns on packaging and printed matter.

Client: **Opentable**
San Francisco, California, USA

Agency: **Turner Duckworth**
San Francisco, California; and London, UK

The Challenge

A nationwide online restaurant-reservation network, Opentable.com offers restau-rants the opportunity to reach a broad audience of potential and repeat local and out-of-town patrons. The website also gives viewers a chance to place and con-firm advance reservations at more than 1,400 popular and high-end restaurants and hotel chains around the clock without making a phone call and without pay-ing a service charge. As an added incentive, member patrons can also earn rewards program points redeemable for meals at participating restaurants. Turner Duckworth's biggest challenge in designing this identity was to communicate with both the potential patrons and the participating restaurants.

Turner Duckworth used an effective device of color contrast to illustrate Opentable.com's service—finding an available table in the crowd.

The Process

The San Francisco design team worked closely with the client to create a con-cise creative brief and then went to work developing a small number of signifi-cantly different designs. The Turner Duckworth design process dictates that every work in progress is sent to the studio's sister office in London. There, the project is critiqued, edited, and improved before it is presented to the client. As a result, the selected logo—four disks symbolizing dining plates with a clean typographic treatment—changed very little after the initial presentation.

The Result

Turner Duckworth's logo received rave reviews from the client. In fact, one of the greatest compliments the studio received for its efforts was the referral of new clients by Opentable.com's CEO.

Braue's classically styled seaside resort logo design highlights the hotel's distinctive tower and reflects the Mediterranean influences inherent in its design.

Perhaps the ultimate test of an illustrative logo, the hotel's tower icon is emblazoned right next to the tower it represents.

Client: **Hotel am MedemUfer**
Otterndorf, Germany

Agency: **Braue: Branding & Corporate Design**
Bremerhaven, Germany

The Challenge

Situated on the North Sea, Lower Saxony is a traditional German summer vacation destination. The Hotel am MedemUfer in Otterndorf is a small luxury hotel nestled in the heart of the town, on a canal, and not too far from the region's spectacular coastline and beaches. Here, Braue's designers faced a straightforward challenge: to incorporate the architecture of the hotel's distinctive tower into the logo and to reflect the Mediterranean influences in the hotel's design.

The Process

There's no substitute for experience. To design this identity, Braue's designers spent time at the hotel and in the town. Then they scoured three major German cities, conducting intensive on-site research at other hotels and resorts. The result of these efforts was a logo that instantaneously gives the viewer a glimpse of what can be found at not just the physical location but the surrounding destinations.

The Result

Visitors and guests truly begin to appreciate Hotel am MedemUfer's logo when they see it next to the real tower it represents. This same illustrative materials also serve as the basis for the hotel restaurant's identity.

The logo's waterline juxtaposes nicely with beach images in the hotel's brochures. It also carries the feel of the property across all of the hotel's other printed material.

The Caffè Bene logo conveys cappucino's richness and pleasure in color, saturation, and lettering style. The designers manipulated an existing font to fit their vision.

Client: **Caffè Bene**
            Otterndorf, Germany

Agency: **Braue: Branding & Corporate Design**
            Bremerhaven, Germany

The Challenge

Long before Starbucks emerged to reshape the face of the coffee business, German villages, towns, and cities were already lined with coffeehouses and cafés. When the owner of the Hotel am MedemUfer decided to open Caffè Bene inside his hotel, he called Braue design—which was only natural, as Braue had created the identity for the hotel itself. But now the design team had to create an identity that would stand alone—above other coffeehouses—and integrate into the hotel's existing corporate design architecture.

The Process

There is no Starbucks in Otterndorf or Bremerhaven—yet—but the brand is so strongly identified with the current global wave of coffeehouses that Braue design immediately identified it as one brand to study. They turned up dozens of others through intensive research on the Internet as well as in three major cities in Germany; their goal was a solution that did not shout "Starbucks clone."

The principle behind their design was to convey the richness and pleasure of a cappucino in the color, saturation, and style of the lettering. The designers based the typographic design on an existing font, then manipulated it until it fit their vision for the brand. After eight or ten hand-sketched roughs were winnowed to three or four strong ideas, the final concept and one alternate were fine-tuned and presented.

The Result

Opening in May 2003, Caffè Bene's non-Starbucks image and prime hotel location has already attracted both hotel guests and a loyal local audience, exceeding the owner's expectations.

This detailed logo is surprisingly strong in small sizes, as on the side of this coffee cup.

The logo's red ribbon background not only binds the logo elements together but also helps it stand out on printed matter. Here, the iconic coffee cup works as a screen-back for the café's menu.

Client: **OneWorld Challenge**
Seattle, Washington, USA

Design: **Hornall Anderson Design Works, Inc.**
Seattle, Washington

The Challenge

The OneWorld Challenge represented the Seattle Yacht Club in the 31st America's Cup race in 2002. Bringing together a remarkable team of designers, boat builders, and sailors hailing from seven nations, the OneWorld brand had one mission: to win the world's oldest sports trophy in the name of global oceanic health—a critical issue of marine stewardship that needed the media positioning and influence that this prestigious yacht race can afford. Hornall Anderson Design Works (HADW) was commissioned to visually convey the importance of this sailing team's quest and commitment.

The Process

With the core communication of environmental awareness and responsibility, the HADW design team set out to visually convey feelings of earth, sea, and sky. They chose illustrations of easily recognized icons: a bird, the horizon, and a fish. The team did not have to communicate any submessages about the racing team's sponsors, which included veteran America's Cup technology partners SAIC and the Ford Motor Company, outfitter Polo Ralph Lauren's RLX line, and a number of telecommunications investors. The HADW team simply concentrated on issues greater than winning the world's most coveted trophy.

The Result

Versatility was the crowning glory of HADW's design solution. The brand identity was successfully applied to OneWorld's shore base signage, training boats *USA 51* and *USA 55*, the main racing hull, support craft, banners, shirts, hats, bottled water packaging, stationery program, brochures, collateral, and other promotional materials. Not an easy task.

Bright orange creates a natural counterpoint to the blue logo on OneWorld's letterhead and collateral materials.

OneWorld's petroglyphic solution stands up to the challenge of being identifiable from a great distance.

Client: **3M Company**
Minneapolis, Minnesota, USA

Agency: **Franke + Fiorella**
Minneapolis, Minnesota

The identity for the 3M Championship Senior Golf Tournament preserves the sponsoring company's brand integrity, placing the 3M mark front and center as evidence in this invitation for the event.

The Challenge

When Minneapolis-based 3M Company became the title sponsor of the 3M Championship Senior Golf Tournament, the corporate giant knew a brand mark with strong consumer appeal would bolster sales of branded merchandise. Although the event was part of the Senior PGA Tour, 3M needed to preserve its own integrity. The design solution could not be perceived as altering or enclosing the 3M logo. That was the challenge Franke + Fiorella faced when they were commissioned to create this specialty brand.

The Process

Competitive audits of other sponsored event marks were performed and analyzed, followed by intensive design exploration. The process led to the development and refinement of an identity in which the familiar 3M brand is paired with a dynamic circular illustration of a golfer.

The Result

Held at the Tournament Players Club of the Twin Cities golf course, designed by Arnold Palmer and Tom Lehman, the 3M Championship Senior PGA Golf Tournament took place over six days in August 2003. To remind loyal PGA fans and 3M customers who came to watch Wayne Levi win a $1.75 million purse with a birdie on the 18th hole, the 3M Championship logo was implemented on everything from newsletters, advertising, the official website, billboards, golf balls, tickets, customer invitations, and a wide range of branded souvenir merchandise.

Newsletters (pictured here), website, billboards, golf balls, tickets, and even branded merchandise supported the promotional efforts for this 3M-sponsored event.

A dynamic circular illustration of a golfer creates a strong point of difference when paired with the familiar 3M brand in this identity for a major PGA Tour stop.

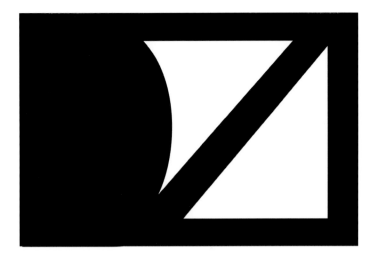

de Zigne Institute.

A logo that reached both English- and Japanese-speaking audiences was the mandate issued by Tokyo's hip fashion emporium de Zigne Institute (DZI). The design solution surrounds the brand with an air of culture and intelligence that speaks of the store's art gallery and philosophy without alienating consumers who just want to shop.

Client: **DZI: de Zigne Institute**
Tokyo, Japan

Agency: **Staple Design**
New York, New York, USA; and Tokyo, Japan

The Challenge

Located in Tokyo's Urahara district, de Zigne Institute (DZI) offers stylish fashions targeted to Japan's fashion-conscious youth market. Like many Japanese retail venues, the store also houses an art gallery that features modernist installations. DZI's owners called on Staple Design to create a logo that could be readily appreciated by both English- and non-English-speaking consumers.

The Process

Staple Design's team wanted to surround the brand with an air of culture and intelligence without alienating customers who just want to shop. They decided to approach the project by developing a typographic abstraction. Since the greater portion of the target audience does not speak English, the letters themselves wouldn't hold any particular significance to the viewer, but if the initials were arranged as a typographic art form, they would attract the right audience. A raw black-and-white palette allows the play on the letters *D*, *Z*, and *I* to speak for itself.

The Result

Young Japanese consumers are extremely style conscious; in fact, brands often serve as a badge of taste and distinction as much as the apparel and accessories themselves do. The success of the design was quickly determined by this audience, who loved sporting the bold logo in the streets when it was implemented on the store's shopping bags.

Crystalware is an old-fash-ioned and even cliché cate-gory in the mindset of many consumers. Stuart Crystal realized it suffered from visual age and a stagnated brand identity, which was refreshed to appeal to a young audience with a sleek identity created by Lewis Moberly.

Client: **Stuart Crystal**
Stourbridge, UK

Agency: **Lewis Moberly**
London, UK

The Challenge

To most consumers, the crystalware category is old-fashioned and even cliché. One of the top traditional brands, Stuart Crystal, realized it was suffering from visual age and stagnated brand identity. The distinguished manufacturer of fine crystal asked the Lewis Moberly creative team to formulate a modern, sophisti-cated identity—a radical move in the industry that includes Waterford, Wedgwood, and other brand names. The change was spurred by the need to move the company into territory with a new target audience. The Stuart brand needed not only to invite a younger target consumer audience but also appeal to the new breed of British interior designers, whom the company hoped to attract.

The Process

The Lewis Moberly design team developed several ideas geared to presenting crystal as a sleek, evocative form capable of attracting its intended new audi-ence of designers and consumers. Working through a variety of type treatments, the team oriented the final design so that it would not put off or distract potential product designers from creating original crystal designs.

The Result

The refreshed Stuart Crystal logo helped bring a dying brand back to life. This modernized identity is now proudly displayed by retailers and has spawned its first designer range—Jasper Conran at Stuart Crystal. Lewis Moberly also crafted this line extension, which has become the UK's top-selling crystal brand. Both the main Stuart Crystal identity and its ancillary have won numerous awards, including the Design Week Corporate Identity Award and a British Design and Art Direction silver nomination.

Captured on shopping bags and packaging, Stuart Crystal's new identity serves as a banner for an upscale, hip young audience of designers and consumers.

Stuart Crystal's first designer line extensions, created by Jasper Conran, received a similar sleek identity. The line has become the United Kingdom's top-selling crystal brand.

Client: **Alfred Dunhill**
London, UK

Agency: **Lewis Moberly**
London, UK

The Challenge

A purveyor of fine formal wear, clothing, leather goods, and accessories, the Alfred Dunhill brand is firmly established as the epitome of British luxury for men. But to extend its presence across an expanded product line, the company needed to modernize its identity and give it an edginess that would appeal to a new and younger audience. Dunhill called on Lewis Moberly to update its image for the launch of its newest men's fragrance, d.

The Process

Branding at its best builds from within. In presenting this new fragrance, the Lewis Moberly team selected the name d and confidently presented it to the client as the essence and hero of the company's line extension. The final visual solution became obvious: Play on the minimal yet distinctive style so popular among younger British consumers but echo the established Dunhill proprietary typeface and treatment. The result yielded a bold, confident presence that plays well in multiples on store shelves. Unlike the existing Dunhill fragrance line, the new image appeals to the younger British male audience, which is attracted to minimalist modernity over tradition.

The epitome of British luxury goods for men, Alfred Dunhill needed an updated image that would appeal to a younger generation of customers demanding modernity and edginess from the products they embrace.

To launch Dunhill's new
men's fragrance, d, Lewis
Moberly played on the minimal yet distinctive style so
popular among younger
British consumers but
echoed also the established
Dunhill proprietary typeface
and treatment. This bold,
confident presence plays well
in multiples on store shelves.

The Result

The d fragrance brand positioning and packaging resonated exceedingly well with
both new and existing Dunhill consumers. Carving out a new market without dam-
aging an existing one is always a challenge; Lewis Moberly met this one with ease.

Shopping.com™

A company merger created the world's ultimate shopping experience— Shopping.com. The company's dedication to providing an accessible, informative resource for shoppers on numerous levels inspired the creation of Shoppy, a character that figures prominently in the brand's identity.

Client: **Shopping.com**
Brisbane, California, USA

Agency: **Turner Duckworrh**
San Francisco, California; and London, UK

The Challenge

Since 1999, DealTime and Epinions helped millions of consumers make better shopping decisions. In April 2003, the companies merged into Shopping.com to create the world's ultimate shopping experience. Shopping.com reflects the combined vision and expertise of the leading shopping search engine and the leading consumer reviews and ratings platform, respectively.

The company offers consumers the opportunity to apply the power of information to making the best shopping decisions. Since this is a technology brand that exists almost exclusively on the Web, it was particularly important to give it an approachable personality people could relate to.

The Turner Duckworth design team used everything they had learned over the past four years of online shopping design research and development, including what people like (and dislike) about shopping; how they use the Internet in their everyday lives; and why they would rather buy online than offline. Shopping.com is the result of the team's efforts.

The Process

The design team worked with the client to produce a concise, creative brief. Then they developed a handful of significantly different designs. Part of the Turner Duckworth design approach is to share the process while the work is in progress. The San Francisco team sent the concepts to the London office, where the work was edited and improved before it was sent to the client. The selected logo—featuring a checkbox converted into a happy shopping bag— changed very little after the initial presentation.

The Result

The Shopping.com logo was such a success, the Turner Duckworth team was asked to design a soft-toy logo. As Shopping.com's chief operations officer stated, "The identity continues to be the most praised element of our relaunch. People love Shoppy."

Shoppy comes to life in an animation created for the relaunch of the merged brand. The figure conveys the message of a happy experience, frame after frame.

Shopping.com's mascot has become so popular among consumers that the character appears on promotional items like those pictured above. A soft-toy Shoppy has also been produced.

pure hair.

Bergman Associates steered clear of cliché visuals such as flowers and sprigs of herbs to convey the message that Purehair offers pure organic plant and flower aromatherapy hair care products for a modern culture.

Client: **L'Oréal**
New York, New York, USA

Agency: **Bergman Associates**
New York, New York

The Challenge

Natural ingredients and fresh botanical essences are anything but cutting edge in the beauty market, especially in the hair care category. When the ARTec division of L'Oréal launched its Purehair line—professional (salon)-use-only shampoos, conditioners, and styling products—it needed to establish an immediate point of difference in the saturated market. Even in salons, upscale hair products vie for shelf presence: the brand has to visually convey the promise of quality suggested by the salon owner's choice of products.

The Process

In the beauty industry, brands are usually customized to appeal to a narrow target audience. But Purehair's focus is deliberately broad, appealing to salon clientele of all ages, genders, and ethnicities. In fact, the brand bills itself as "cross-generational" line. Veteran brand builders in the beauty category, the Bergman Associates design team knew that clichéd visuals such as flowers, herbs, and feminine, scriptlike type treatments were out of the question when developing a solution. Consequently, the team focused on communicating the purity of the ingredients and the uncomplicated sensual experience each customer enjoys.

The Result

Concentrating on a simple, modern statement, the Bergman Associates team executed the brand's name in a clean sans serif type treatment. The team split the name, using solid and screened type to improve legibility. The tagline—Pure organic plant and flower aromatherapy for a modern culture—verbally complements the visual message.

The launch of this cross-generational hair care line was so successful it's given birth to the Pure Shop by L'Oréal ARTec. Line extensions have reached beyond the basics, offering consumers the latest in styling breakthroughs such as finishing shines, fortifying gels, and sense-soothing aromatherapy candles for use in the salon and at home.

The Purehair brand and packaging leaps out at stylists and customers alike, earning shelf presence with its simple, direct visual message which was executed to appeal to clientele of all ages, genders, and ethnicities.

PHILOSOPHY
DI
ALBERTA FERRETTI

For the opening of her first Philosophy boutique in the United States, Alberta Ferretti wanted an identity that would fuse with the existing Ferretti logo, which resonated with a strong point of difference to her audience of fashion-conscious women who frequent the small, upscale shops of New York's SoHo district.

Client: **Philosophy di Alberta Ferretti**
Milan, Italy

Agency: **Bergman Associates**
New York, New York, USA

The Challenge

Italian fashion designer Alberta Ferretti's haute couture line of clothes and accessories have graced the modeling runways for years. Philosophy di Alberta Ferretti interprets the designer's sense of flowing elegance for the ready-to-wear market. For the opening of her first Philosophy boutique in the United States, Ferretti wanted an identity that would fuse with the existing logo. The identity had create a strong point of difference with an audience of fashion-conscious women who frequent the small, upscale shops in New York's SoHo district, looking for fashions that spell individualism and timelessness in no uncertain terms.

The Process

The Bergman Associates design team addressed this challenge by employing a typographic approach that spoke of self-confidence, intelligence, youthful spirit, and individuality. The letterspaced sans serif type treatment offers familiarity to Ferretti's loyal followers, who can immediately recognize the designer's signature identity. It also offers potential patrons a strong promise of what they can experience in the boutique and how they will feel in the designer's ready-to-wear line.

The Result

The Philosophy di Alberta Ferretti boutique in New York's SoHo has been a resounding success, joined by stores in China, France, Italy, Japan, Kuwait, South Korea, Taiwan, the United Kingdom, and the United Arab Emirates. Throughout the world, the logo appears on letterhead, packaging, the ready-to-wear line's labels, signage, and the company's website, signaling fashion-conscious women to take notice.

The U.S. flagship store's image attracts Ferretti's loyal followers, who can immediately recognize the designer's signature identity, and offers potential patrons a strong promise of what they can experience in the boutique and how they will feel in the designer's ready-to-wear line.

Client: **Liz Earle Vital Oils**
Isle of Wight, UK

Agency: **Turner Duckworth**
San Francisco, California, USA; and London, UK

The Challenge

Created by Liz Earle Cosmetics, Vital Oils is a range of essential oil–based aromatherapeutic products that promote well-being. Poured into the bath and used as body sprays, the products are intended to induce comfort, harmony, bliss, and other emotions in the user. Turner Duckworth faced the challenge of developing a mark that would express the simple but magical therapeutic qualities of these highly concentrated essential oils to consumers.

The Process

Since the products are bottled in tiny vials and packaged in equally small boxes, physical dimension had a huge impact on design exploration and refinement. The logo had to be clean and simple and work in a very, very small size. The graphic solution was a single drop of oil falling from a star. The accompanying type treatment was executed in a highly legible sans serif font. The bright color palette expresses the therapeutic effects that can be obtained: Gold symbolizes comfort, green represents harmony, and rosy red depicts bliss.

The Result

Printed in satin silver foil and embossed so the droplet has a jewellike three-dimensional effect, Vital Oils' image has an ultrapremium look. Since its launch in 2003, the Vital Oils line has attracted a loyal following of British consumers, who shop for the product at Liz Earle's Union store and upscale department stores as well as online.

A single drop of essential oil falling from a star says it all about Liz Earle Cosmetics' line of Vital Oils.

Poured into the bath and used as body sprays, the Vital Oils products are intended to induce comfort, harmony, bliss, and other emotions in the user. The packaging is color coded to express the therapeutic effects that can be obtained: Gold symbolizes comfort, green represents harmony, and rosy red depicts bliss.

vital oils
the essence of wellbeing
comfort vital oils for the bath

vital oils
the essence of wellbeing
harmony vital oils for the bath

vital oils
the essence of wellbeing
bliss vital oils for the bath

bliss
vital oils for the bath

sensual sandalwood
heady jasmine
beautiful rosewood
fortifying black pepper
joyful ylang ylang

Client: **Union**
Isle of Wight, UK

Agency: **Turner Duckworth**
San Francisco, California, USA; and London, UK

The Challenge

Liz Earle Cosmetics produces the Naturally Active Skincare product line, made from a synthesis of natural ingredients and state-of-the-art science. Featuring skin cleansers and toners, body- and sun-care treatments, vital oils, and shimmery makeup products, the line appeals to an upscale audience looking for a natural way to maintain a youthful, radiant appearance. The United Kingdom–based beauty company decided to launch a flagship retail outlet and called on Turner Duckworth to develop both the name and its visual identity.

The Process

Turner Duckworth's brand development team selected the name Union because it not only described the union of nature and science but also because the shop space is conveniently located along Union Street on the Isle of Wight. As one team member remarked, "Once in a blue moon a project like this comes along, and the process of arriving at a solution is simple. The name was thought of over a beer with the client, and the logo was the first idea on the layout pad. However we tried, we couldn't do better than that. Then came the enjoyable task of carefully crafting the type. If only more could go this easily."

Visually, the solution was equally simple. The design team selected a lowercase serif type treatment and then joined the first two characters together, allowing them to share the same upstroke. A soft, verdant color palette reinforced the message of the cosmetic company's commitment to using natural ingredients.

The Result

Opened in 2003, Liz Earle's Union shop has attracted numerous local customers as well as tourists visiting the Isle of Wight. The simple sea-fresh logo has been a resounding success.

The Liz Earle Cosmetics flagship store on the Isle of Wight is situated on Union Street. Its brand addresses the union of nature and science, as portrayed in this typographic brand identity.

Branded on its signage, the Union store speaks of Liz Earle Cosmetics' synthesis of natural ingredients and state-of-the-art science in its Natural Skincare line, which features skin cleansers and toners, body- and sun-care treatments, vital oils, and shimmery makeup products that appeal to an upscale audience looking for a natural way to maintain a youthful, radiant appearance.

Client: **Boa Housewares**
Croydon, UK

Agency: **Turner Duckworth**
San Francisco, California, USA; and London, UK

The Challenge

Boa's first—and highly successful—product was the Boa Constrictor, which helps unscrew tight jar lids. The company wanted to expand its range to include homeware products such as knives, knife blocks, and bread-cutting boards. It called in Turner Duckworth for a brand review.

The studio advised the client to keep its distinctive name and leverage its value in the marketplace. The challenge was to refer to the company's successful past without limiting its future in product lines that go beyond the kitchen.

The Process

Turner Duckworth showed the company a handful of solutions that played on the name and referenced Boa's high-end design style. The final design solution is subtly based on the shape of intertwining snakes and includes the tagline "Formed for function." The simple, strong graphic device is legible regardless of its application: molded into the products, printed on packaging and shipping cartons, or incorporated into the stationery program and collateral materials.

The Result

Boa's new identity and packaging won many design awards, as have the products, designed by Priestman Goode. The completed project is a great example of collaboration among graphic designers, product designers, and, of course, an enthusiastic client. In the first six months of trading, over one million units of the first Boa product have been sold.

A solution subtly based on the shape of intertwining snakes includes Boa's tagline—"Formed for function"—which creates a simple, strong graphic device that's legible regardless of its application.

Boa's identity had to leverage its strong equity based on its highly successful product, the Boa Constrictor, which helps unscrew tight jar lids. Expanding to homeware products, Boa had to address its successful past without limiting its future in product lines that go beyond the kitchen.

NATURALLY ACTIVE
SKINCARE
LIZ EARLE

Client: **Liz Earle Naturally Active Skincare**
Isle of Wight, UK

Agency: **Turner Duckworth**
San Francisco, California, USA; and London, UK

The Challenge

A leading British beauty company, Liz Earle Cosmetics developed a new line of skincare products—Liz Earle Naturally Active Skincare—that combines natural ingredients and scientific technology. The challenge was that the line's proprietary logo had to hint at the science and stress the concepts of nature and natural ingredients.

The Process

Turner Duckworth followed their design exploration down a path of symbols that led to the combining of a plant leaf and a molecular whirl to create a flower, sending a message that freshness and radiance are the results a user can expect from the products. When the solution was presented to the company's two directors, there was a transformation from worry and anticipation to total relief and joy at the solution. As one studio member remarked, "We definitely felt like we'd just made their day."

The Result

Turner Duckworth's design solution for Liz Earle Naturally Active Skincare is hot foil stamped onto product packages and printed on company signage, retail signage, gift packaging, advertising, and merchandising. It also appears in animated form on the company's the website and in multimedia presentations. Since its launch in 2003, the line has been picked up by such upscale British stores as Browns, Atelier, and Esporta, and it is featured at Liz Earle's flagship Union store.

Liz Earle Naturally Active Skincare combines natural ingredients and scientific technology. Its logo stresses the concepts of nature and natural ingredients combined with scientific technology, employing familiar elements such as a leaf and an atom.

Applied to sleek, foil-stamped packaging, the Liz Earle Naturally Active Skincare identity translates in many forms, including an animated presence for the Web and a multimedia presentation for potential retailers and customers who visit the company's retail outlets.

NOURISHING
BOTANICAL BODY CREAM

NATURALLY ACTIVE
BODYCARE
LIZ EARLE

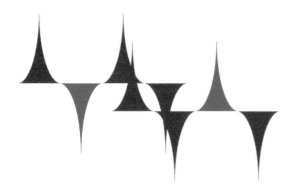

KIRNA ZABÊTE

CLOTHING / ACCESSORIES / HOME

A multilevel iconic presentation demonstrates Kirna Zabête's department-store approach to retailing youthful, hip products ranging from fashion and toys to makeup and appliances.

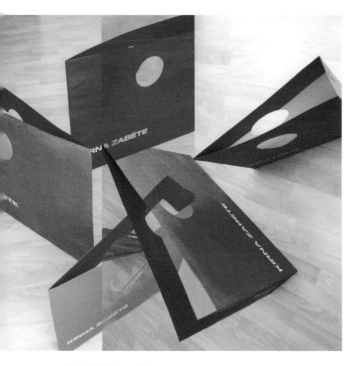

Kirna Zabête's brand identity speaks a dynamic language that's even translated in the shape and design of the store's shopping bags.

A series of fanciful sub-icons were developed to address Kirna Zabête's youthful spirit and individualistic attitude.

Client: **Kirna Zabête**
New York, New York, USA

Agency: **Bergman Associates**
New York, New York

The Challenge

Department stores are frequently viewed as mainstream shopping experiences, places where consumers can purchase anything from appliances and makeup to fashions and toys. Located in the heart of New York's unconventional SoHo district, Kirna Zabête offers its boutique-oriented patrons a department-store experience that's anything but mainstream. The owners wanted a multipart logo that dynamically communicated its mission to offer unique clothing, accessories, and homewares in a single location.

The Process

Bergman Associates made its first visual statement by developing an sleek, modern icon, executed in a red and gray palette, that tells of the store's many levels and offerings. The type treatment—a strong, wide sans serif—speaks a dynamic language as a stand-alone on shopping bags or in tandem with the icon. A series of fanciful subicons was developed that speak of the store's youthful spirit and individualistic attitude.

The Result

Carrying products created by new designers as well as established names like Jean-Paul Gaultier and Balenciaga, Kirna Zabête has earned its name in adventurous fashion among fashion-conscious men, who are its biggest audience. Bergman Associates' complex identity serves as a badge of excellence on the store's letterhead, packaging, signage, and website. The Kirna Zabête identity was also branded on hundreds of items, and it even inspired the shape of the store's shopping bags.

Client: **Ixora Rye**
Rye Brook, New York, USA

Agency: **The Missive**
New York, New York

The Challenge

Designer Thom Stoelker created the interior for a floral shop situated in New York State's Westchester County. Ixora is named after a rare wildflower found in the Malaysian jungle and caters to the large Asian professional and corporate executive population that lives in the area. Stoelker wanted a colorful and graphically powerful identity for the store. He also wanted the logo to have flexibility while maintaining some connection to the store's square floor plan.

During the design process, The Missive did not have access to the store, had no communications with the owner, had only a black-and-white photocopy of the actual ixora flower, and had only four hours in which to divine a solution. The overwhelming challenge was that the client needed the design immediately—in 4 hours. Because the store is 1.5 hours away from The Missive's office, the team could not visit the space ahead of time. As Thom Stoelker is an industry celebrity, it was understandable that they would not be able to meet him for even a moment, but the reward for executing a successful conclusion to the project would payoff in referrals and recognition. So The Missive team worked from a black-and-white photocopy of the actual ixora flower to divine a solution in record time.

The Process

The intrepid logo designer listened carefully to the interior designer's instructions and descriptions. He incorporated the store's square layout as a design element coupled with a sketch of the exotic ixora as a graphic focal point. The store name was rendered in raw, hand-drawn letters and accompanied by the tagline "Exotic Asian Garden," executed in a stabilizing Baskerville font. The muted green and red color palette conveys a fresh atmosphere.

The Result

Since the store opening, Ixora's logo has appeared on its stationery, packaging, business cards, and price and souvenir tags. It has been a perfect complement to the atmosphere and integrity of the company.

Created in less than half a day, Ixora Rye's logo evokes an Eastern influence in an area populated by a professional Asian audience.

Powerful and distinctive, the Ixora identity displays the store's square layout and its Asian orientation in its stationery program, which is pictured here.

Exemplifying an upbeat personality and the positive energy female baby boomers seek in products, Keds' Grasshopper identity addresses the desire of wearers to have fun.

Client: **Keds Corporation**
Lexington, Massachusetts, USA

Agency: **Desgrippes Gobé Group**
New York, New York, USA

The Challenge

Keds' classic white sneakers have been a staple in women's and girls' wardrobes for over 80 years. The Massachusetts-based company recently decided to expand its market range through its Grasshoppers line extension, aimed at women over age 45. Baby boomers comprise a huge market segment that's devoted to comfort. They demand comfort from the jeans they wear and from the shoes they put on their feet. However, Grasshoppers needed to be perceived as more than affordable, comfortable footwear. To gain market share, the brand had to communicate a message that the wearers have fun.

The Process

During the exploratory process, the Desgrippes Gobé team drew the conclusion that the Grasshoppers brand is about enjoying life. The Grasshopper woman has an upbeat personality, a flair for fashion, and an on-the-go lifestyle. The team sought to appeal to this target entity by combining a fanciful illustration of a grasshopper atop blades of grass and a feminine but sturdy type treatment. The soft green color palette adds vitality and freshness to the brand's overall appearance.

The Result

The refreshed Grasshopper brand has heralded a major audience transition for this popular Keds brand, attracting the huge female baby boomer market. Packaging is the primary vehicle for the Grasshopper brand's visual identity.

The grasshopper and blades of grass that make up the brand's identity speak of the outdoors on terms that its consumers clearly understand.

Branded on its packaging, labels, and collateral materials, the Grasshopper brand communicates accessibility, affordability, and flair to its on-the-go female audience.

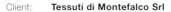

Tessuti di Montefalco S.r.l.
06036 Montefalco (PG), Italy
Via Ringhiera Umbra, 25
Tel./Fax +39 0742 378119

The quality of the fabric and a town landmark figure largely in providing this classic logo with a sense of place and heritage.

Client: **Tessuti di Montefalco Srl**
Montefalco, Italy

Agency: **Studio GT&P**
Foligno, Italy

The Challenge
Textiles are more than the practical fabrics people use every day to make clothes, cover furniture, and form an array of household items ranging from pillow shams and napkins to curtains and seating. The textile industry spans the world of needs, desires, and fantasies that consumers appreciate on an aesthetic level as well as an economic one. Tessuti di Montefalco has a chain of retail shops that sell a range of fabrics that appeal to connoisseurs and practical shoppers looking for materials and patterns to fill their needs.

The Process
A town landmark figures largely in Studio GT&P's icon for Tessuti di Montefalco, which offers the viewer instance recognition and a sense of place. Set in an oval seal and complemented by a classic serif type treatment, the emblem speaks of the rich history of the weaver's art and the artisan guilds that perfected the craft.

The Result
A sense of place, tradition, and quality were all achieved in Studio GT&P's successful brand identity for the Tessuti di Montefalco.

The Tessuti di Montefalco identity speaks of the store's legacy as an art guild with its bronze store-front plaque.

An identity that speaks of tradition, style, and affordability, Tessuti di Montefalco's logo is worn like a badge of honor by patrons, who carry this shopping bag.

TESSITURA
PARDI

The mastery of the jacquard weaving art and the shuttle that runs across the loom, represented by punch-hole designs similar to a player piano's music rolls, are the elements that inspired this classic logo design for Tessitura Pardi.

Client: **Tessitura Pardi Srl**
Giano dell'Umbria, Italy

Agency: **Studio GT&P**
Foligno, Italy

The Challenge

Jacquard fabrics were an invention of the nineteenth-century industrial revolution. Complex patterns could be woven by machines without the assistance of more than a single master weaver, thanks to an inspired use of punch-hole designs that are read like the music rolls of a player piano. Silks, linens, cottons, and woolens could all be designed with intricate patterns and sold for a reasonable sum, thanks to Joseph Jacquard's remarkable unpatented system. Tessitura di Pardi employs this nearly two-centuries-old system to produce linens and other fabrics for fashion and interior designers. The company needed a sophisticated logo that conveyed the jacquard process as its sole point of difference to a discerning, upscale audience that spans the globe.

The Process

Studio GT&P researched the rich history of jacquard weaving techniques and distilled it in a single visual message: the motion of the shuttle. The design team further refined this form as a silhouette, which they employed in Tessitura Pardi's visual brand.

The Result

A lush photograph of a shuttle nestled in an array of draped fabrics and spools of thread finishes and complements the story when paired with the logo on packaging, collateral materials, and sample books. Appealing to a huge international audience of shoppers who frequently order online, an animated version of the logo and its distinctive shuttle icon also appear on the opening page of the company's website.

The shuttle and draped jacquard fabrics work as subordinate, illustrative components throughout the Tessitura Pardi identity program.

The MF+P team researched Estonian history, then fused Scandinavian and Germanic styles to create an Estonian brand that visually dominates other superpremium vodkas on bar and store shelves.

Client: **Türi Vodka**
Miami, Florida, USA

Agency: **Margeotes|Fertitta + Partners**
New York, New York, USA

The Challenge

The United States is the world's largest premium vodka market. Over the past five years, this exploding category has segmented and evolved into premium, superpremium, and ultrapremium sectors. Dozens of new brands are launched annually, causing fierce competition for shelf presence in stores and bars. Most new brands have followed the tall, frosted-glass model to gain consumer interest. But one new entry—Türi Vodka—has taken a refreshing new route. Türi Vodka's defining element is its country of origin, Estonia. The challenge to the creative team at Margeotes|Fertitta+Partners (MF+P) was that few Americans know where Estonia is, and even fewer know anything about this former Soviet satellite, which is situated between Russia and Finland. The mark had to communicate the persona, history, and aesthetic of this mysterious place.

The Process

The MF+P design team's research revealed that Estonia had experienced self-rule in only 30 years of its centuries-old history. Even after a dozen years of independence from Soviet rule, Estonia's culture demonstrates little discernible national identity, drawing mostly from influences adopted in previous centuries under German and Swedish rule. The MF+P team chose to embrace this point of difference, developing a brand image that had a clean, simple Scandinavian structure with Germanic Gothic touches—a new Estonian aesthetic.

The Result

The thought behind the mark itself led the way to the creation of the vodka's packaging. The name is boldly featured on the front, while the logo is embossed on the bottle's distinctive metal-encased neck. The result is an elegant and distinctive package that begs to be picked up.

Client: **Kazi Beverage Company**
Portland, Oregon, USA

Agency: **Hornall Anderson Design Works, Inc.**
Seattle, Washington, USA

The Challenge

The flavored alcoholic beverage is a relatively recent phenomenon in the spirits industry. It offers a young target audience premixed, single-serving alternatives to conventional beers, wines, and cocktails. Kazi Beverage Company identified a niche in this flooded category: developing a beverage that would appeal to men and come in flavors other than hard lemonade and Long Island iced tea. However, it had to look like the kind of drink a guy wouldn't be embarrassed to consume at a party. To craft Kazi's visual point of difference, the company called on Hornall Anderson Design Works (HADW).

The Process

The HADW design team set out to create a cool, masculine, contemporary look that was slightly edgy. They focused on 20-something males and developed a readily identifiable six-pack carrier. The team added lighthearted touches throughout the design solution. Filtered photographs of cocktails illustrate both the packaging and supporting materials. The brand's upside-down *A* resembles a stemmed cocktail glass. Pickup lines are printed on the inside of each bottle label, and the beverage's taglines drive home the brand's essence: "cocktail in a glass" and "liquid entertainment."

The Result

The client loved the direction of the design, so Kazi's strongly masculine brand image was employed on both beverage flavors, six-pack carrier, point-of-sale and collateral materials, signage, and in-store displays.

To market flavored alcoholic beverages to men in a female-dominated market, HADW used bold type and imagery as well as pickup lines and an earth-toned palette, which is traditionally avoided for food and beverage packaging.

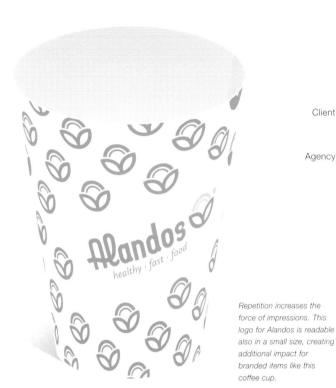

Repetition increases the force of impressions. This logo for Alandos is readable also in a small size, creating additional impact for branded items like this coffee cup.

With a sun and leaves employed to symbolize life and health, the Alandos logo is a radical departure from the circus-strength branding tradition of the fast-food market, epitomized by McDonald's.

Client: **Alandos Healthy Fresh Food**
Offenbach, Germany

Agency: **H2D2, Office for Visual Communication**
Frankfurt am Main, Germany

The Challenge

The German fast-food market reached a value of nearly 5 billion marks in 2002. The obvious favorite menu item is the burger, which accounted for 63.4 percent of sales. McDonald's was the front-runner, owning a 31 percent market share. However, a new trend is emerging as customers shift away from high-fat foods toward healthier alternatives, just as they are doing in the United States and Canada. Offering a healthy fast-food alternative in the lucrative German marketplace, the Alandos healthy fresh food franchise company wanted a visual presence that would communicate the quality of food preparation and natural ingredients it offers at reasonable prices while evoking the warm, human ambience of its store interiors.

The Process

The H2D2 team worked closely with the store's interior designer, exploring visual interpretations and type treatments that communicate the concepts of "natural" and "human" to a targeted health-conscious, youthful audience. The H2D2 team first experimented with handwritten typography, which looked personal and individualistic but wasn't serious and succinct enough to convey confidence and trust in the product. The team's eventual solution was to produce two logos: a horizontal version and a circular version. Both images combine the warmth and pleasant nature of handwritten type and a confident, modern italic, a fresh green palette, and a stylized icon that depicts fresh leaves growing in the sunshine.

The Result

The Alandos simple brand image clearly communicates fast food but also, more importantly, fresh and healthy fast food.

CIBO NATURALS

Client: **Cibo Naturals**
Seattle, Washington, USA

Agency: **Daigle Design**
Bainbridge Island, Washington

The Challenge

Cibo Naturals is a line of ready-to-eat flavored cheeses, pestos, dips, and condiments made with all-natural ingredients. Targeting not only health-minded consumers but "foodies" as well, the line is marketed to both retailers and food-service companies. When Daigle Design was commissioned to refresh Cibo's logo and packaging, its goal was to create a simple yet organic identity that symbolized the fresh ingredients used in the products.

The Process

After a careful, competitive review of food shelves, Daigle Design chose to depart from Cibo's old vine-shaped identity, opting instead for an elegant, illustrated basil leaf that would be legible on branded containers, labels, and boxes. The type treatment was chosen as a strong counterpart to the flowing, stylized leaf.

The Result

Since the logo's unveiling, the line's distribution has considerably expanded. The logo itself has received national design award recognition.

A redesign of Cibo Naturals' previous ivy logo, this basil leaf incorporates an organic, illustrative style with a strong textual counterpart.

The golden basil leaf logo is highly visible in a variety of packaging colors. Its curve gives the impression of the leaf settling in place.

Client: **Pace International**
Seattle, Washington, USA

Agency: **Hornall Anderson Design Works, Inc.**
Seattle, Washington

The Challenge

To improve their appeal on produce shelves, fresh fruits and vegetables are frequently washed and polished before they are packaged for presentation. Pace International is the manufacturer of a cleaning and coating product that achieves this goal. But how does a product that makes produce look better appeal to its target market? Most competing products are packaged in sterile, cold-looking packages. The Hornall Anderson Design Works (HADW) team took on the challenge of finding and implementing a more compelling visual point of difference.

The Process

The previous visual brand had incorporated scientific and chemical elements into its design. The HADW team imbued Pace International's new identity with a friendly and accessible spirit. The team combined elements that spoke to both the cleaning and coating agents as well as the fruits and vegetables themselves. The fresh palette of bright citrus colors conveys the healthiness of the treated produce, emphasizing how Pace's products help preserve freshness.

The Result

Unlike its predecessor, the new Pace International identity diminishes the typically negative response to the use of a chemical product, increasing its appeal to a potential new client base of health-minded produce merchants. Naturally, the new image was applied to the client's stationery program, signage, barrel labels, and other packaging. The company was also a sponsor of a cycling team, so Pace International commissioned cycling jerseys with the new fresh image, gaining further exposure.

To brand Pace International, a manufacturer of produce cleaning and coating agents, HADW combined elements of both with the fruits and vegetables themselves.

On printed matter, the fresh palette of bright citrus colors conveys the healthiness of treated produce and emphasizes how these products help preserve freshness.

On packaging, the fruit theme is played on through product-specific imagery that also serves as a safeguard to ensure that each solution is used on the right fruit.

Tamarind, the first Michelin-starred Indian restaurant, wanted a nontraditional identity for its prepared foods. Lewis Moberly created this contemporary yet accessible brand.

Client: **Tamarind**
London, UK

Agency: **Lewis Moberly**
London, UK

The Challenge

Ethnicity doesn't always allow for crossover marketing or expansion into new and more profitable territory, even in the expanding packaged foods industry. For example, Indian products are typically branded and presented in a cliché form involving ornate lettering and decorative motifs against a garish color palette. What if your brand has broken consumer expectation barriers on one level and needs to express that message on extensions and sub-brands?

Tamarind is the world's first Indian restaurant to receive a coveted Michelin star, an honor it has retained for three consecutive years as of 2003. The London venue, situated in the upscale Mayfair district, has set a new agenda for modern Indian cuisine. Like many brand-name restaurants, Tamarind developed a line of high-quality at-home products, based on contemporary Indian recipes. But its early packaging did not attract potential retailers in the lucrative UK marketplace. Lewis Moberly was contracted to identify and develop a visual brand that would resonate with British consumers and retailers, who in the past few years have radically raised their expectations of the taste and quality of prepared foods.

The Process

After careful industry research and testing, the Lewis Moberly team identified a strong design direction: simplicity, modernity, and relevance. The team chose a strong visual point of difference guaranteed to set the product line apart from its competitors. A bold upper- and lowercase sans serif typeface was selected, set against a dark background. The red bindi—a jewel adornment worn on the face by Indian women—is the witty, edited clue added to attract Britain's many aficionados of Indian cuisine and culture.

The Result

Tamarind's new identity was an immediate success with UK retailers, who had previously delisted the product line from their shelves. Consumers who were frequent restaurant patrons were readily attracted to the packaged goods extension, and new consumers were easily drawn to the product line's credibility and visual accessibility.

For packaging, Lewis Moberly let the logo drive the design, continuing with highly abstracted traditional Indian patterns and bold red, white, and black.

Client: **Refreshments Brands**
Danville, California, USA

Agency: **Turner Duckworth**
San Francisco, California; and London, UK

The Challenge

The spirits industry has been booming since the resurgence of cocktail culture in the mid-1990s. From vodkas and rums to fruit-based liqueurs and flavored malt beverages, spirits categories are emerging and growing. A new entry in this burgeoning marketplace, Truce is the first single-serve cognac, vodka, and juice drink to be marketed in the United States. Turner Duckworth was called in by Refreshment Brands to develop both the name and the beverage's brand identity. The challenge was to create a clean, effortless brand that appealed to a 21- to 35-year-old target audience.

The Process

During the naming phase, the Turner Duckworth team discovered that when France's Emperor Napoleon and Russia's Czar Alexander met in the 1800s, they liked each other and called a truce between the two nations. Since French cognac and Russian vodka are an unexpected pairing of ingredients, the name *Truce* fit very well.

The studio presented three logo and packaging concepts ranging from a design inspired by the Napoleon and Alexander story to a modern design that resonated well with a younger audience. The black-and-white treatments of the product's name are interlaced on a silver-gray backdrop. The package design also employs a rich maroon color palette. The clients—who were not part of the target demographic—preferred the more traditional design but selected the modern solution based on the studio's advice. The final design was only slightly enhanced after the initial presentation.

The Result

The brand launched in early 2004 alongside Refreshment Brands' other new entry into the ready-to-drink beverage category, Envy. Truce's modern logo now appears on packaging, sell sheets, point-of-sale materials, and promotional items that are handed out to potential distributors, off-premise retail establishments, and restaurant and bar owners. It's still too early to tell how it will affect the success of the brand, but expectations are understandably high.

Running vertically on labels, the logo is instantly readable—and right side up to viewers on both sides— when someone drinks out of the bottle.

Client: **Fairtrade Labelling Organizations International (FLO)**
Bonn, Germany

Agency: **Interbrand**
London, UK

The Challenge

Fairtrade Labelling Organizations International (FLO) is the worldwide Fairtrade standard-setting and certification organization. FLO permits over 800,000 producers and their dependents in more than 40 countries to benefit from labeled Fairtrade certification. FLO guarantees that products sold anywhere in the world with a Fairtrade label marketed by a national initiative conform to Fairtrade standards and contribute to the development of disadvantaged producers. FLO retained Interbrand's London branch as brand consultants. The organization wanted clarification of internal brand issues as well as a strategic platform. It needed a clear vision, mission, and values as well as support for its decision to develop a single certification mark for the organization's seventeen national initiatives.

The Process

The Interbrand creative team conducted a visual audit of the organization's existing communications materials. They discovered the organization was represented by 10 diverse certification marks that were all meant to convey the same standard, values, and goals from different perspectives, some working better than others. It also had presence in marks that represented seven ancillary initiatives. The team advised FLO that if its vision was to change the world and the way the world does business, it needed to internationalize and strengthen its visual presence. There was some resistance to this recommendation from members who felt more protective about their established marks than others, but the team successfully argued in favor of alliance over autonomy in its final presentation—an approachable and confident abstract visual that represented the exuberance of the small farmer being given a good price for harvested crops and the consumer buying better-quality products that were fairly traded.

The Result

Applied to food and beverage packaging as well as its dedicated website (www.fairtrade.net), the new FLO visual identity is replacing old certification labels at varying speeds throughout the world. The Fairtrade Labelling Organization International's mission and goals are rapidly gaining global acceptance. One in four nations now recognize the Fairtrade certification label. Sales of fairly traded food products continue to rise even among the world's largest supermarket chains. Dedication to fair trade has also expanded to the hospitality industry: Starbucks now makes all its coffee drinks with Fairtrade-certified coffee beans. Interbrand's solution was a finalist in the Design for Good category of the Design Effectiveness Awards.

The Fairtrade Labelling Organizations International (FLO) icon creates a series of intentional elemental images—a road toward prosperity, a farmer waving, and a green leaf—all created by the same abstract.

To brand products from around the world, the FLO logo had to be able to support text in a variety of languages while retaining its visual impact.

The FLO icon is applied with and without its textual element on a wide variety of collateral materials.

Client: **Carlton & United Brewing**
Melbourne, Australia

Agency: **Cato Purnell Partners**
Richmond, Australia

The Challenge

Beer has gone light over the years in response to consumers' desire to reduce overall caloric intake. To meet that growing demand, Carlton & United Brewing planned the launch of a new, premium light lager that boasts a full beer flavor, dispelling the notion that light beer has little taste. The brewery named this new product Sterling. The brand's identity was intended to carry positive historical connotations of excellence and quality while positioning the beer as a respectable alternative for the growing audience of light beer drinkers.

The Process

Cato Purnell Partners developed a signature type treatment for the brand, employing a strong script for the name and adding shadow to accentuate its visibility on shelves and on the bar. A star, frequently employed as a symbol of excellence, in this case serves as an emblem and a guarantee that the product is made with the finest ingredients and craftsmanship.

The Result

The Sterling brand was launched in late 2003 throughout Australia and, with the help of the bold identity, successfully found its appeal among a male audience of beer drinkers who want an economical, tasty beverage.

To brand Sterling, a new light lager, Cato Purnell's team created a strong script name with shadow to accentuate its visibility on shelves and on the bar.

A star is a traditional symbol of excellence. Here, it serves as an emblem and a guarantee that the product is made with the finest ingredients and craftsmanship.

Client:

Caledonia Australis Wine Company
Leongatha, Australia

Agency:

Cato Purnell Partners
Richmond, Australia

Caledonia Australis' thistle and grape icon pays tribute to the Scots who first settled the region.

The Challenge

Over the past three decades, the wine industry has expanded beyond the borders of France, Italy, and Spain. Regions not known for wine production in the past have gained a substantial foothold on the international market. Chile, Portugal, Australia, Canada, and even China have garnered the attention of enthusiastic international wine connoisseurs.

To gain brand recognition in a superheated market such as the wine industry, it takes a strong visual identity that evokes quality, sophistication, and heritage to gain the interest and trust of increasingly educated wine consumers.

The Caledonia Australis Wine Company is a privately held Australian producer that bottles premium and superpremium wines from its own Pinot Noir and Chardonnay vineyards, located in an area that has soil and growing conditions unsurpassed outside of France.

When the vineyard was first opened for distribution with award-winning vintner Martin Williams at its helm, it called on Cato Purnell Partners to craft an identity that would speak of the vineyard's long history and mission to create quality wines.

The Process

The Cato Purnell design team discovered the name Caledonia Australis' long, rich history through extensive interviews with vineyard executives. Inspired by a landscape that reminded him of his beloved Scotland, explorer and squatter Angus McMillan was so moved by his first view of eastern Victoria from Mount Macleod in 1839, that he "...named it at the moment Caledonia Australis."

Caledonia is an archaic name for Scotland. And Australis is the original name for the southern Australian region now known as Gippsland. Together, the names describe both the location and the heritage of the area outside of the Gippsland town of Leongatha, where numerous vineyards grow the high-quality Pinot Noir and Chardonnay grapes used in Caledonia Australis Wine.

The thistle has long been recognized as a symbol of Scotland. And the Cato Purnell design team linked it with a stylistic rendition of grapes on the vine to form a timeless icon. Pairing this accessible identity with a classic type treatment with both elegant script and a sturdy serif, the team created a logo that would immediately tell consumers the wine has an evocative history as well as great taste.

The Result

When Caledonia Australis's 2000 wines were debuted in 2002, they met with major acclaim among wine reviewers, who not only evaluate wine for its taste, but for its packaging. Both Cato Purnell's label and its contents won over this discerning spectrum of defacto judges even before it was given major kudos in sales by the public.

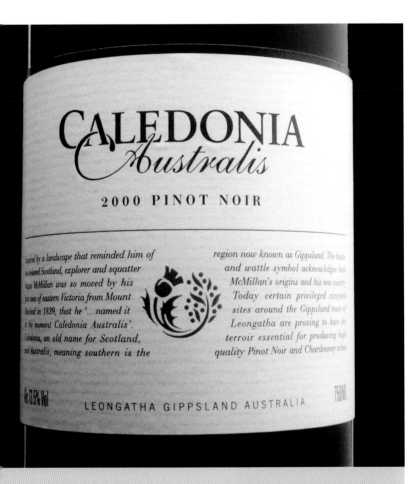

The true elegance of the Caledonia Australis type and brandmark becomes apparent when they are in place on packaging. The curves of the Australis A speak of vines as they link through the A and E in Caledonia.

Client: **Canpull**
Croydon, UK

Agency: **Turner Duckworth**
San Francisco, California, USA; and London, UK

The Challenge

Have you ever broken a fingernail or cut yourself while opening a pull tab, easy-open can? There must be a few consumers who have done so—enough to inspire Canpull's creators to develop and market a device that makes opening a can a breeze. During the product's development phase, the owners asked Turner Duckworth to design the packaging.

The Process

The Turner Duckworth team placed a C in a circle to represent an easy-open can top. The proprietary type treatment was developed from that stylized letter.

Fortunately, in this case the name clearly conveys what this innovative product does. The challenge for Turner Duckworth was to create a mark that helped the consumer realize its purpose. The design team observed that an easy-open can's ring-pull looks like a letter *C*, so they placed the letter in a circle to complete the symbolic representation of a can top. That stylized letter became the launch point for the proprietary type treatment. Additional solutions were also developed for the team's first presentation to the client. In the end, the team's preferred treatment became the client's choice.

The Result

When packaging is a company's single most important form of communication, it's fair to say that strong sales figures are, in part, due to a successful design solution. Canpull's launch has netted excellent returns for its creators and numerous creative design awards for its logo designers.

BLUEBERRY

BLACKCURRANT

CHERRY DROP

Canpull's packaging plays off the same functionality as the logo, symbiotically emphasizing the brand and the product.

vitamin^{GLACÉAU}water

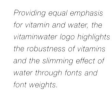

Client: **Glaceau Vitaminwater**
New York, New York, USA

Agency: **Lloyd & Company**
New York, New York

Providing equal emphasis for vitamin and water, the vitaminwater logo highlights the robustness of vitamins and the slimming effect of water through fonts and font weights.

The Challenge

As consumers have become increasingly aware of the health benefits of hydration and the detriments of soft drinks, the bottled water industry has boomed. Of course, most products are simply spring or distilled water with packaging as the sole point of difference. When Glaceau created vitaminwater, it designed the product to target the heart of consumers' health-related interest in bottled water. The challenge that Lloyd & Company faced was placing equal emphasis on vitamin and water in the identity.

The Process

The Lloyd & Company design team applied its standard logo design criteria—simple, clean, powerful, and distinctive. The challenge of creating an icon to represent vitamin in balance with water made it clear that a typographic brandmark would be more effective than an icon. After the design team was happy with the design internally, they tested the image externally before they finalized it and presented it to the client.

The Result

Glaceau Vitaminwater's branding is used primarily on packaging but also on stationery, signage, and a wide range of collateral materials. Though Lloyd & Company has received plenty of positive feedback about the design, they prefer simply to point to the brand's huge success.

In small print, as seen on this business card, the emphasis shifts to the word vitamin, drawing the viewer's eye. On the water bottles, color plays an essential part in branding the individual flavors. These colors play along the bottom of the business cards and other printed material, representing the entire line.

energy

tropical citrus (c+ginseng)

we, the makers of this product, hereby rebut any offers by any professional sports leagues to become "the official water" of anything. although this is a great alternative to sports drinks, we do not believe in succumbing to commercialism. unless, of course, there's a lot of cash. then we'll talk.

vitamins + water = what's in your hand

one sip, swig or gulp may result in boycott of other beverages.

energy brands inc. whitestone, ny 11357 800 746 0087 www.drinkbetterwater.com bottle design and label: TM and ©2003

20 FL OZ • 591 mL

vitamin^{GLACÉAU}water
nutrient enhanced water beverage

revive

fruit punch (b+potassium)

for best results, mix with individuals showing signs of sluggishness and apathy.

warning: if severe procrastination occurs, buy a whole case.

active ingredients: see contents on label. inactive ingredients: see contents on your couch.

vitamins + water = what's in your hand

one sip, swig or gulp may result in boycott of other beverages.

energy brands inc. whitestone, ny 11357 800 746 0087 www.drinkbetterwater.com bottle design and label: TM and ©2003

20 FL OZ • 591 mL

Client: **Penta Star Srl/Adamantis**
               Perugia, Italy

Agency: **Studio GT&P**
               Foligno, Italy

The Challenge

Specialty alcoholic beverages are hitting their prime, now that cocktails, wines, and beers are achieving a demand level that hasn't been seen in nearly three decades. To gain the attention of distributors, restaurateurs, bar staff, and consumers, new entries into the alcoholic beverage industry must display and sustain a point of difference that cannot be equaled or contested.

Created by Penta Star SRL, Adamantis is a specialty spirit: an Italian grappa. It's a neutral spirit, like vodka, that's made with grapes instead of grain or potatoes. The name Adamantis is derived from the Latin word for diamond, *adamantis*. Studio GT&P's job was to convey the messages of quality and uniqueness that are implied by an iconic diamond.

The Process

Since the brand needs to appear not only as a title signature but also as embellishment on various portions of the packaging, Studio GT&P created a stand-alone icon that adds a diamond to a highly stylized, open-faced capital *A*. The same icon is serves as a focal point in the type treatment. Both treatments were rendered for use in black-and-white and in gold foil.

The Result

Embodying premium values such as modernity, elegance, and style, the Adamantis logo and icon appears on its bottles, packages, shipping cartons, hang tags, sell sheets, shelf talkers, collateral materials, and point-of-purchase materials. The brand will be rolling out for international distribution to upscale restaurants, bars, and retail outlets in 2004.

Adamantis is Latin for "diamond." To convey Adamantis' quality, Penta Star SRL paired an elegant capital A with an iconic diamond.

Rather than positioning the A-and-diamond icon at the front of the text logo, the designers used the middle A in Adamantis. The strength of this symmetry reveals itself on packaging and labels.

The two roosters in San Potente Agriturismo's icon suggest strength, vitality, and the firm's strong link with nature, while the type is refined and legible, reflecting the company's high-quality products.

The logo makes a strong base on labels and packaging for the farm's extra-virgin olive-oil, preserves, and other products.

Client: **San Potente Agriturismo SAS**
Foligno, Itlay

Agency: **Studio GT&P**
Foligno, Itlay

The Challenge

The worldwide consumer demand for low-cholesterol, natural, high-end imported food ingredients has changed the way food producers of artisanal ingredients view both the marketplace and their identities. Meanwhile, travelogs such as *A Year in Provence* have birthed a whole new segment of gastro- and agrotourism. San Potente Agriturismo, nestled among Umbria's vineyards and olive groves, is a farm that makes extra-virgin olive oil as well as jams and other regional produce. The estate also offers farm holidays in a variety of luxurious bucolic accommodations. San Potente Agriturismo needed a brand that appealed to both the flourishing imported foods market and an equally impressive and competitive tourism industry that wants focused destinations. The challenge Studio GT&P faced was creating an icon that would spell out the company's dual message of destination and high-quality product in one image.

The Process

Studio GT&P's design team opted for a brand that would hold its strength across a multicultural, global target audience. The two roosters in the brand's icon suggest strength, vitality, and the firm's strong link with nature, while the type is elegant and instantly legible.

The Result

The Internet has helped open the doors to new and repeat bookings to this beautiful property in Italy's Menotre Valley. The owners believe the new logo for San Potente Agriturismo as well as the website Studio GT&P created for them has contributed greatly to an increase in reservations as well as a jump in the sales of the estate's olive oils, jams, and other products.

Reversed out, the logo's color becomes the background for this Umbrian destination's website.

*Daigle Design crafted the
Auction for the Arts logo in
building block style. The
Amoeba Rain font imparts
a raw, typewritten effect
reminiscent of a manuscript
or movie script.*

Sixth Annual
Auction
for the
Arts

Saturday, November 8th

**Clearwater Casino / Slahal Ballroom
Suquamish**

Fabulous Food and Fun!
5-7 pm Silent Auction & Drinks
7-9 pm Live Auction & Sumptuous Dinner
Live Music, Door Prizes & Valet Parking

Fantastic Auction Items
Vacation trips, dinner parties, tours, art in all media, wines,
entertainment, and more

Fun That Funds the Arts!
Procedes benefit Bainbridge Arts and Crafts (BAC),
Bainbridge Island Arts and Humanities Council (BIAHC),
and Bainbridge Chorale

**TICKETS AVAILABLE
at www.ARTSHUM.org,
Bainbridge Island Arts and Crafts and at Art Soup**

Limited Seating, Unlimited Fun!
Call for your invitation or more information
206.855.9692

Client: **Auction for the Arts**
Bainbridge Island, Washington, USA

Agency: **Daigle Design**
Bainbridge Island, Washington

The Challenge
Supporting community arts and humanities on Bainbridge Island, the Auction for
the Arts is an annual event that raises funds through ticket sales, a live auction,
and a silent auction of donated vacation trips, dinner parties, artwork, wines,
and entertainment. For five years, Bainbridge Arts & Crafts and Bainbridge Island
Arts & Humanities Council were the auction's primary beneficiaries. In 2002,
Bainbridge Chorale joined in the event. A new identity was needed to reflect
this addition without showing favoritism to any single organization.

The Process
The Bainbridge Island–based studio Daigle Design took a playful approach to this
design challenge, literally. Rather than attempting to portray each participant's
discipline, the designers crafted a logo out of building blocks, positioning the letters *ARTS* inside each square. The typeface Amoeba Rain gave the overall look a
raw, typewritten edge reminiscent of a book manuscript or the script for a play.

The Result
Supporters took notice of this lively brand and responded with increased ticket
sales and generous donations, making the event an overwhelming success. In
addition, the Auction for the Arts logo received national design award recognition
and is being used for a second year.

*Type-only and stand-alone
icon logo variations allow
the Arts logo to perform in
a variety of layouts.*

Especially in continuing education, the brand message has shifted from "future alma mater" to "accessible and relevant." The Nanyang Technopreneurship Center communicates the essential message with a rising social gesture.

Client: **Nanyang Technopreneurship Center**
Singapore, Singapore

Agency: **ThinkingCouch Interactive**
Singapore, Singapore

The Challenge

The tides of academia are changing. Educational institutions are finding ways to attract postgraduates back to school to enhance their learning and improve their ability to succeed in the workplace. When Nanyang Technological University launched a new postgraduate diploma program that targeted budding entrepreneurs, they called on ThinkingCouch Interactive to develop a brand image that would appeal to both undergraduates and the general public. The program, entitled Nanyang Technopreneurship Center, had to reflect its university lineage in a friendly, approachable way while communicating the bold and independent nature of entrepreneurship.

The Process

The ThinkingCouch team considered solutions that would convey trust and reliability in association with a modern education center that cares to take a daringly different academic approach. They zeroed in on the human element behind the center's mission of providing training, discipline, and networking opportunities with experienced lecturers and speakers—most of whom are successful businesspeople and venture capitalists—for future entrepreneurs.

The Result

The design solution focuses on a stylized human figure surging forward. The bold, contemporary typeface treatment and strong color palette further convey the educational program's dynamic nature. The final identity has been remarkably well received by both students and the public, who quickly associated its presence with reliability, trust, and professionalism.

NABS's previous logo communicated the charity's mission to lend a hand, but it employed a punk-era medium—graffiti on an open palm.

The new NABS logo juxtaposes two speech bubbles—one open and the other filled—to form an N.

Client: **NABS**
London, UK

Agency: **Lewis Moberly**
London, UK

The Challenge

The National Advertising Benevolent Society (NABS) is an organization founded after the World War I as a charity for members of the advertising industry. Nearly a century later, NABS now serves as a charity benefiting the entire marketing communications industry. Because of its age, NABS needed to refresh its identity and leverage its true relevance to a younger target audience of communications professionals. Lewis Moberly was contacted to address this visual revival, bringing NABS into the twenty-first century with a presence that would defy the assumption that it was nothing more than a "retirement home for ex-advertising people."

The Process

The last time the NABS identity had been refreshed, it conveyed a punk-era message: An open human hand presented the organization's hand-printed acronym. Although it communicated the charity's mission to lend a hand, the design didn't address its ability to bring people together one on one, an omission Lewis Moberly sought to address. A space for a question in an upper speech bubble is answered in the lower bubble by the word NABS. Together, the pair of bubbles form the initial *N* in NABS.

The reply dialogue balloon on the backs of NABS business cards come with possible replies that are meant to open the lines of communication.

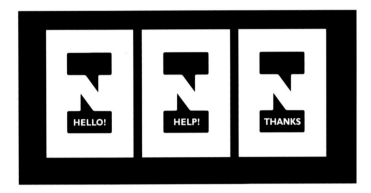

The NABS letterhead reveals the dialogue balloons that outline the NABS logo, by employing this detail as a motif. This is one logo that's strong enough to stand up to the biggest white space without getting lost.

The Result

NABS now has a visual language that invites participation, thanks to the Lewis Moberly team. The identity and logo were launched in June 2001, coinciding with the start of a recession in the communications industry—the very sector from which NABS required increased donations. Despite the economic downturn, NABS and its initiatives have had a phenomenal impact within the industry. Corporate donoations have increased by 20 percent. A portion of this achievement is attributed to the new identity.

The logo itself has received numerous industry kudos, including a 2003 British Marketing Design Award, a 2002 Bronze Clio, and a 2002 Bronze in the New York Festivals.

To retain the Restaurant School's established market while rebranding the newly accredited college, Murphy Design incorporated a script capital from the old brand.

Client: **Walnut Hill College**
Philadelphia, Pennsylvania, USA

Agency: **Murphy Design**
Philadelphia, Pennsylvania

The Challenge

The Restaurant School had trained students for careers in the hospitality industry since 1974. When it recently received accreditation to offer bachelor's degrees, administrators decided it was time to rebrand the school. First, they changed its name to Walnut Hill College to reflect the accreditation. To successfully make such a radical transition, select elements of the old identity had to be retained intact: points of familiarity that would retain the loyalty of alumni and existing patrons.

Even though the campus is situated in urban West Philadelphia, the school administrators wanted to employ a walnut tree as its symbol.

The Process

Murphy Design's exploratory process uncovered close connections between the school's new name and the requested walnut tree symbol. Besides its location on Walnut Street in Philadelphia's Walnut Hill district, the tree is a universal symbol for learning and growth—core values of this educational institution.

The school's maroon and silver color palette and script typeface were the old elements Murphy Design had to incorporate into the new logo to maintain a connection to the old Restaurant School logo. But to characterize the solidity and respectability needed in an educational institution's identity, the script was limited to initial caps in the classic, elegant type treatment.

The Result

Flexibility was key to the logo's great success. Applied to all communications, the new mark was also branded on aprons, chef coats, and other student equipment.

Walnut Hill College's stationery system makes full use of the symbolic connection between the color palette and the walnut tree itself

ReSOurces for SuCCeSS

The WHEEL

After experimenting with numerous images of wheels and gears, Murphy Design created this fun, funky, colorful image to appeal to an undergraduate target audience.

Client: **University of Pennsylvania, Office of College Houses and Academic Services**
Philadelphia, Pennsylvania, USA

Agency: **Murphy Design**
Philadelphia, Pennsylvania

The Challenge
The Wheel is the name of the academic and student support services initiative created by the University of Pennsylvania's Office of College Houses and Academic Services. Consisting of numerous programs such as Resources for Success, the Wheel needed its own visual identity—one that could be used as a stand-alone image and as an iconic reference in conjunction with other subbranded programs. The university wanted this image to be fun, funky, and colorful to appeal to its undergraduate target audience.

The Process
Murphy Design initially explored numerous images of wheels and gears. Because the icon would never be seen as a totally isolated graphic element, shapes were tested and developed simultaneously with a brochure design. A point of difference was finally achieved when the design team focused on the letter *W*. Set in a circle, the calligraphic letterform serves as a signature for the typewriter-like treatment of its own name and for each of its subbranded programs.

The Result
The Wheel's identity debuted on a brochure that was distributed throughout the campus in the autumn of 2003. Further implementation is still in the conceptual stage.

Client: **CARE International**
Atlanta, Georgia, USA

Agency: **FutureBrand**
New York, New York, USA

The Challenge

Although CARE International is one of the world's largest private relief and development organizations, the public erroneously perceived it as a disaster relief provider that offered short-term aid to individuals. The philanthropic group found it increasingly difficult to engage potential supporters. CARE commissioned FutureBrand to create a new visual expression that would realign the organization's image with its mission and convey its message to a broader audience. The FutureBrand team discovered an additional challenge in the process: Presentations to CARE's board were reviewed by representatives from many regions of the world. Each member had distinctive viewpoints on what was an appropriate symbol.

The Process

After intensive research and numerous presentations and discussions, the FutureBrand team found consensus among board representatives in the presentation of concepts that employed familiar circular forms and hands—symbolic of community and human vitality. The team also presented a number of color palette alternatives. Natural tones were voted most appropriate. Working through this complex process, the ideal identity revealed itself—a circle of hands executed in earth tones.

Organic and gestural in nature, the final brand identity invokes the Earth, Sun, and humanity, creating a striking image that symbolizes the partnership among donors, the organization, and the local participants who were once considered recipients or beneficiaries. It was named the Community of Hands. The new logotype is all lowercase—a departure from its all-caps predecessor that spelled out the organization's outdated acronym. The new treatment reaffirms of the social meaning of the word *care*.

To create a new logo for CARE International that would convey its original mission and reach a broader audience, FutureBrand created this Community of Hands invoking the Earth, Sun, and humanity.

While bold and recognizable, CARE's old logo did not communicate its role as one of the world's largest private relief and development organizatons.

The Result

The FutureBrand team created guidelines for the worldwide transition of the old identity's equity to its new politically and culturally neutral brand. The return on investment was almost instantaneous. There was an immediate increase in donations and in the number of Web hits. Internally, the brand realignment served to reenergize staff members, helping them focus once again on their core mission. FutureBrand's work with CARE has been cited as a case study in rebranding by the Harvard Business School.

On printed matter, CARE's logo adds a touch of brightness and warmth that represents its offer of hope and help.

The Prince of Wales's iconic feathers bring the United Kingdom's number-one charity's target audience a sense of belonging and are seen as a badge of honor. The Wolff Olins team refreshed the existing mark with white lines and a vibrant palette.

Client: **Prince's Trust**
London, UK

Agency: **Wolff Olins**
London, UK

The Challenge

Founded in 1976 by HRH Charles, Prince of Wales, the Prince's Trust is the United Kingdom's number-one charity, helping people ages 14 to 30 realize their potential and transform their lives through training, mentoring, and financial assistance for business startups. To date, the trust has improved the lives of nearly 500,000 people. With the new millennium, the Prince's Trust restructured its organization, establishing separate director and council posts in each of the 12 regions it services in Scotland, Northern Ireland, Wales, and England. The trust asked Wolff Olins to update its identity as part of a two-year brand review as well as to create ancillary identities for its many subdivisions. The team was charged with the creation of a fresh, inspiring visual brand that retained the essence of the trust's history and stature.

The Process

At first, the design team felt that a revolutionary makeover should guide the solution. Therefore, they generated concepts that radically veered from the established brand. After focus grouping and further research, the team discovered most people—especially the target audience—were happy with the charity's royal associations. The Prince of Wales's iconic feathers gave them a sense of belonging and are seen as a badge of honor. The Wolff Olins team then proceeded to refresh the existing mark, applying white lines and a vibrant palette to make the image more contemporary, engaging, and exciting.

The palette carries the brand with messages other than the logo, such as the one on this sweatshirt.

Look at things differently.

Are you living the life you want, or the one you've ended up with? What would you really do if you could choose — and what's stopping you?

The Prince's Trust is about getting people's lives to work better. It's about breaking habits. It's about challenging what's standing in your way. It's about getting on and changing things — helping you to help yourself.

get out of your box

Prince's Trust

The lively colors not only project the logo but also extend its message of vitality.

The Result

This outstanding new mark received a seal of approval from the client—a feat in itself. The team also developed a story to accompany the visual solution that continued the trust's branded mission to "get young people's lives working." Wolff Olins additionally created a set of ancillary icons that the Prince's Trust could apply to internal and external communications, including its website.

Client: **Wisma Mulia**
Jakarta, Indonesia

Design: **ThinkingCouch Interactive**
Singapore, Singapore

The Challenge

The Pacific Rim and, in fact, all of Asia continues to experience an economic surge that's made visible by the frequent introduction of new office buildings and residences. Jakarta, Indonesia, is no exception. An upscale commercial building project situated in this bustling urban environment, Wisma Mulia posed three challenges to the ThinkingCouch Interactive design team when it commissioned them to create a brand identity. The first was a one-month deadline to produce and apply the brand solution in time for an awards ceremony being held in its honor by the American Academy of Hospitality Sciences. The second was to appeal to a target audience that includes multinational Asian Pacific companies as well as international business concerns. And the third was to communicate the literal translation of the property's name (Wisma Mulia means "opulent plaza") to a competitive and urban audience that is bombarded with offerings nearly every day.

The Process

The brand image's theme centers around the timeless and contemporary nature of Wisma Mulia's architecture. The ThinkingCouch Interactive team visited the construction site to get a feel for its presence and interviewed the developers to learn more about their marketing and sales strategy. They committed to developing a dot-matrix-meets-skyline typographic treatment to convey the buildings' high-tech amenities and chose pixelated image treatments to continue the modern motif throughout the program.

The Result

The team also developed and implemented the tagline "created for leaders by leaders" that accompanies the mark, applying both visual and verbal imagery to the building's stationery, signage, collateral materials, and interactive CD-ROM. Both the logo and tagline were well received by the building's target audience, resonating with the demand for a modern approach, international appeal, and professionalism in architectural design and function.

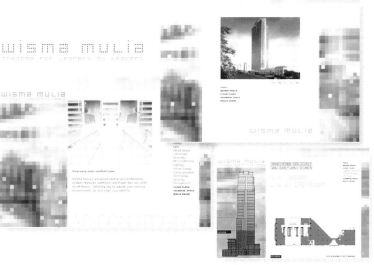

Technology has changed the face of luxury. Script typefaces left with the twentieth century, replaced by digital styles born in electronic music. ThinkingCouch distilled Wisma Mulia's essence—modern comforts and technological amenities—through its sparkling skyline façade.

A waterfront vacation rental home situated on Miller Bay, Salmon Run House is a perfect Pacific Northwest getaway overlooking the prime king salmon run that inspired its name and identity.

Client:

Salmon Run House
Miller Bay, Washington, USA

Agency:

Daigle Design
Bainbridge Island, Washington, USA

The Challenge

A waterfront vacation rental home situated on Miller Bay, Salmon Run House is a perfect Pacific Northwest getaway for families, couples, and wedding parties. The house overlooks the prime king salmon run that inspired its name. The owners wanted an identity that would convey the accommodation's location and sense of serenity, so they called on Daigle Design.

The Process

A colorful illustration of a king salmon was the first element the Daigle Design team settled on when they developed Salmon Run's logo. The challenge came when they began to search for a typeface that would convey the feeling of water splashed by a spawning salmon. Tree Frog was the final choice. It took a number of orientations to decide how to combine these two strong elements into the cohesive visual that became the design solution.

The Result

Salmon Run House's availability was first promoted on the Internet and through a brochure. Daigle Design's logo was implemented in both media as well as the accommodation's stationery program. The image definitely struck a chord with its market. The first booking season was extremely successful, and the logo itself received a 2003 American Corporate Identity design award.

Friday, April 23, 2004

THE BAY   THE HOUSE   ACTIVITIES   RESERVATIONS   DIRECTIONS   CONTACT

WELCOME

Salmon Run House is a waterfront 4 bedroom rental house located on Miller Bay - a king salmon run just 4 miles north of Bainbridge Island. It has everything you need for a short vacation or an extended stay.

The home is perfect for families, couples, friends, business retreats, wedding parties, reunions or weekend getaways. It sleeps 8 people comfortably. Kids are welcome, credit cards are accepted and a 2 night minimum is required.

This 2800 square foot house is close to Bainbridge Island, Poulsbo, Kingston, Indianola, Suquamish and Hood Canal. Instead of staying at a hotel, motel, inn or b&b, make this fully furnished home your special place to stay in Washington.

Employed on its website and printed materials, the identity resonated with potential guests, who embraced the logo and its promise of an ideal leisure destination in its first season.

Sakai Village

A RESIDENTIAL COMMUNITY ON BAINBRIDGE ISLAND

Erected on immigrant Sonoji Sakai's 33-acre family farm, Sakai Village's identity harkens back to its origins and offers viewers insights into the beauty of the natural wetland that borders the site.

Client: **Sakai Village**
Bainbridge Island, Washington, USA

Agency: **Daigle Design**
Bainbridge Island, Washington

The Challenge

A new community situated on Bainbridge Island, off the Seattle coast, Sakai Village has a beautiful legacy. It was originally the family farm of Sonoji Sakai, who had immigrated to the United States from Japan in 1918. Sakai and his wife, Yoshiko, grew strawberries and raised six children on the 33-acre plot. Bordered by open spaces and trails, the new island community is enveloped by a natural wetland habitat that offers residents a serene environment in which to raise a family. The developer commissioned Daigle Design to create a brand identity that would convey the community's natural surroundings of cedar trees with its Japanese legacy.

The Process

The Seattle-area has a rich Asian cultural base and heritage, so it didn't take much for the Daigle Design creative team to focus on and develop a Japanese calligraphic treatment for the Sakai Village identity. The area is also proud of its natural legacies: its temperate rain forest and coastal attributes. This led to the incorporation of the cedar sprig in the finished design.

The Result

The simple Asian-inspired logo received national recognition in 2002 from American Graphic Design Awards. The developer, Bainbridge Island–based Landmark Homes, is clearly pleased with the Sakai Village logo. It appears throughout its website, on all Sakai Village signage, and on all printed materials.

Seattle's rich Asian cultural base and heritage as well as its temperate rain forest surroundings meld into the cohesive message seen in Sakai Village's signage and collateral materials, pictured here.

INSITE WORKS

ARCHITECTURE
SITE DESIGN **DEVELOPMENT**

Client: **InSite Works**
Albuquerque, New Mexico, USA

Agency: **Hornall Anderson Design Works, Inc.**
Seattle, Washington, USA

Using an I-beam as the infrastructural support, InSite Works' identity addresses the architectural firm's mission to create sound structures from environmentally friendly modern materials.

The Challenge

InSite Works has a reputation as an atypical full-service architectural firm. The company creates structures that utilize a variety of environmentally friendly materials. One such example is its use of Rastra, a concrete form system made from cement and recycled postconsumer plastics, in its design for Albuqerque's Desert Springs Church. InSite Works needed an identity program that reflected its eco-conscientious use of building materials and its thorough attention to detail.

The Process

The I-beam is the strongest piece of infrastructure support in a building. The Hornall Anderson Design Works (HADW) design team decided to use this as the focal point in InSite Works's visual identity. The image is also intended to symbolize the firm's support of its clients. On occasion, InSite Works actually assists in generating the necessary funds for a client's project. The HADW design team purposefully notched out the I-beam symbol on the firm's cards to emphasize this significance.

The Result

InSite Works's identity has been implemented on its stationery program, miniature CDs, and drafting sleeves. Completing the brand's overall look, an engraved metal card was designed to serve as a multifunctional piece. The client is thrilled with the way the cards look when attached to proposal covers. Printed stickers are sometimes applied to the surface for presentation purposes.

InSite Works' identity, branded across its entire presentation, stationery, and collateral program, reminds viewers that the firm supports its clients from start to finish.

النخلة

A massive luxury housing development that's being constructed off the coast of Dubai, the Palm needed an identity to be legible in both English and Arabic.

Client: **The Palm**
Dubai, United Arab Emirates

Agency: **FutureBrand**
New York, New York, USA

The Challenge

The Palm is a massive luxury housing development that's being constructed off the coast of Dubai, one of the United Arab Emirates. From the air, the man-made islands, Jumeriah and Jebel Ali, and their surrounding atolls each form a palm tree silhouette under a crescent-shaped arch. Set for completion in 2004, this government-sponsored project posed a number of problems to the FutureBrand design team charged with creating its brand. The image had to portray the extraordinary engineering and construction feat of the islands themselves. The final logo also had to reflect a lifestyle brand that could not be immediately experienced but promised the epitome of luxury. Finally, the brand had to be presented in English with an alternate Arabic version: a rarity in the United Arab Emirates, where identities present both English and Arabic type treatments.

The Process

The FutureBrand team developed hundreds of options that spanned several design ranges. These initial proposals were vetted down to four solutions, each expressing a distinct aspect of the Palm's brand strategy. The winning candidate was personally selected by Sheikh Mohammed bin Rashid Al Maktoum, Crown Prince of Dubai.

The Result

The Palm's identity was a huge success. When the project launched in May 2003, the island sold out all of its villas in a matter of hours, setting a record for Dubai real estate sales and establishing a new standard in the region for real estate branding and marketing solutions. In addition to its phenomenal business success, The Palm project has received worldwide recognition, and the branding work has won numerous regional and international awards, including American corporate identity awards and applied arts/multimedia awards for the Web and video work. The Palm and its affiliated clients have become FutureBrand's long-term partners across numerous projects since the success of the Palm launch.

The Palm's unique shape—a man-made island constructed in a shape of a palm tree—is echoed in the iconic palm frond shown here on its website.

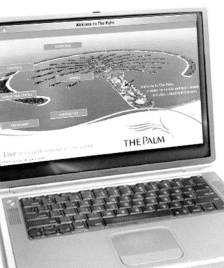

Promises of luxury, elegance, natural beauty, and leisure accentuate the Palm's identity program, which employs magnifications of these elements throughout its collateral program.

ORCA

Client: **ORCA**
Bremerhaven, Germany

Agency: **Braue: Branding & Corporate Design**
Bremerhaven, Germany

The Challenge

Since the dawn of construction, the building industry's mantra has been "measure twice, cut once." Technology is changing that adage. With virtual construction allowing engineers, architects, and designers to walk through simulations of a completed structure before breaking ground, a decade from now builders may be advising their clients to "look before you build." The advantages for new construction, renovation, and retrofitting are enormous.

ORCA is an acronym for one German company's core services: object management, room/space coordination of units in mechanical engineering, CAD/CAM solutions, and administration/documentation. Braue's challenge was to capture all of this in a single mark and to make virtual industrial construction accessible to prospective clients, with an overall futuristic and distinctive appearance.

The Process

The Braue design team researched the industry online and conducted extensive target audience interviews. They also studied the company and analyzed the common theme of ORCA's various services before coming up with a type treatment that speaks volumes. The highly stylized letterforms look as if the viewer is seeing them on a magnified monitor screen. The pale green against a medium gray palette also conveys that message.

The Result

Under this cohesive identity, the company grew from four original partners to a 60-person corporation, becoming one of Germany's leading virtual engineering companies.

Virtual construction has changed the way engineers, architects, and designers see a structure before ground is broken. ORCA employs this revolutionary digital solution in the services it provides for its clients. The company's logo appears as it would magnified on a monitor screen.

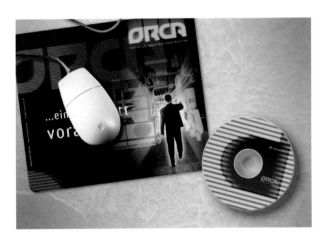

Used on the company's presentation and collateral materials, ORCA's logo also serves as an effective marketing tool on promotional mouse pads and CD-ROMs.

Three hues differentiate Novoscreen's three thickness levels of sun protection: Vista, Balance, and Spectra.

Novoscreen's innovative screen fabric is demonstrated for use in the production of vertical blinds and roller blinds in a state-of-the-art display, branded with its sleek logo.

Client: **Novoscreen**
Bremerhaven, Germany

Agency: **Braue: Branding & Corporate Design**
Bremerhaven, Germany

The Challenge

Sunscreen goes far beyond skin. The sunscreen industry for businesses is growing and rapidly changing. Braue's challenge was to establish Novoscreen's identity as a new subbrand of Sunprotex, a highly successful screening fabrics manufacturer.

The compamy's logo system was needed for the R+T 2003, the world's largest and most important trade show for roller shutters, doors, gates, and storm and sun-protection products. Braue had three weeks to get through the concept, research, competitive audit, design, exploration, presentation, design refinements, final presentation, and production.

The Process

The Novoscreen product line comprises three screen textiles for sun protection in workplaces where computers are used. These textiles are used for the production of vertical blinds and roller blinds. Each of the Novoscreen textiles—Vista, Balance, and Spectra—has a different thickness. Braue visualized this with three rectangles in three different tints. Since Novoscreen is an innovation in this industry, the designers chose a typeface with a modern and futuristic feel and customized the letterforms to fit their goals.

The Result

Novoscreen's brandmark was created to inform prospective clients all over the world about the new sunscreen fabric collection. It proved a tremendous success for this startup company, especially in Asia and Canada.

Novoscreen's identity program employs a futuristic feel and approach to the design of its collateral and promotional materials, direct mail, catalogs, and brochures.

Roofscapes inc. ℠

Green Technology for the Urban Environment

A green alternative to heating and cooling in urban environments, Roofscapes uses its identity to address the beauty that can also be found in this emerging residential and industrial solution to interior temperature and humidity control.

Client: **Roofscapes, Inc.**
            Philadelphia, Pennsylvania, USA

Agency: **Murphy Design**
            Philadelphia, Pennsylvania

The Challenge
Green and *smart* are terms that are entering the mainstream of the building industry. More and more structures are constructed out of economical materials that provide warmth, light, and protection without harming to the environment. Philadelphia-based Roofscapes, Inc., takes this concept a step further, bringing verdant beauty to the roofs of new and existing structures while providing winter warmth, summer coolness, and balanced humidity levels to the interior. The company specializes in the installation and landscape design of green roofs and caters to both residential and industrial developers. The identity for this new launch had to say this message loud and clear in a one- or two-color application and had to adapt easily to both print and digital presentations.

The Process
During the development of the company's promotional brochure, the client asked Murphy Design to create a brand identity. The team explored typographic options for the tagline "Green Technology for the Urban Environment." Visually, this phrase serves as a black earth foundation. The green company name serves as the overhanging rooftop. Using a condensed serif typeface, the logo grows tall and green, helped by the addition of the stylized, leafy swash that emerges from the letter *R*.

The Result
Initially, Murphy Design's solution was implemented on Roofscapes' stationery program, collateral materials, presentation folders, and a PowerPoint presentation. The logo has definitely helped business bloom with orders from new accounts.

Print and collateral materials are unified by Murphy's use of natural paper and images of a "green" environment, further creating a holistic portrait of the company.

An identity created for an independent interior designer, Design Directions Interior Design's logo provides a crisp, memorable brand for this one-person company.

Client: **Design Directions Interior Design**
Los Altos, California, USA

Agency: **Zurek Design**
Easton, Pennsylvania, USA

The Challenge

Anita DeSousa is an independent interior designer who needed a crisp, memorable name and image to represent her one-person company. The challenge faced by Zurek Design's Pamela Zurek was one of distance. The client is based in California—a far cry from Zurek's Pennsylvania studio. However, sometimes relationship and reputation outweigh proximity. DeSouza chose to work long-distance with Zurek because she knew her and knew the quality of her work.

The Process

Together, Zurek and DeSousa selected the name Design Directions for the fledgling firm. Zurek then presented DeSousa with three logo solutions in PDF format via email. Once DeSousa settled on a basic style, Zurek refined six two-color combinations, looking for one that conveyed the critical messages of crisp, vibrant, and professional. A striking blue lavender paired with black offered the most effective solution for the bold, stylized sans serif type treatment, housed in a square.

The Result

Zurek's logo has garnered attention for DeSousa's company. Thanks to the new identity, the business has really taken off. DeSousa recently completed the remodeling of an upscale restaurant, 231 Ellsworth (the name and the address), in San Mateo, California.

Client: **Oregon Power Solutions, LLC**
Baker City, Oregon, USA

Agency: **TAK Designs, LLC**
Baker City, Oregon

Off-grid or supplemental wind power is sweeping the Pacific Northwest, where power sources are at a premium. Oregon Power Solutions' true-to-life style addresses the strength and effectiveness of an old concept driven by new technology.

The Challenge

Off-grid or supplemental wind power has become a viable energy source in the Pacific Northwest, where sweeping winds blow across barren high desert plateaus and access to municipal power sources is at a premium. Oregon Power Solutions is one of many companies harnessing this renewable resource for electrical power. The client wanted to use a windmill image in its identity package, but it did not want to use the true-to-life style, which, in its opinion, others in the industry have overused. The logo also needed to confer not just the name but also a feeling of ecological responsibility as well as messages of an old concept being driven by new technology.

The Process

Beyond these criteria, TAK Design was left to its own devices. The team selected a heavy, classic serif font and stacked the graphic and text in a manner that gives an almost mechanical feel to the identity's overall appearance. They created a stylized icon that depicts an almost straight-on view of a turning wind turbine. To fulfill the client's request for an ecological or "green" message, a blue and green palette was selected. Approximately 15 concepts were developed along these lines before the client made the final selection.

The Result

To date, business cards have been produced on recycled paper stock for this startup company, which is launching its new enterprise in 2004. The client plans to expand the identity's presence when more funding becomes available.

Specializing in the crafting of high-end cabinetry, built-ins, doors, furniture, and millwork for residential, commercial, and institutional markets in the Pacific Northwest and California, Blue Mountain Workshops' identity depicts its mountainous location.

Client: **Blue Mountain Workshops, Inc.**
Baker City, Oregon, USA

Agency: **TAK Designs, LLC**
Baker City, Oregon

The Challenge

Nestled in Oregon's Blue Mountain region, Blue Mountain Workshops specializes in crafting high-end cabinetry, built-ins, doors, furniture, and millwork for residential, commercial, and institutional markets in the Pacific Northwest and California. The 6,000-square-foot facility needed an identity that spoke of its location and its strong presence in the region. This was a challenge, as the iconographic image could not be depicted with cliché imagery.

The Process

TAK Design, also located in Bend, Oregon, took up the task, which carried the additional mandate of using a classic serif typeface in the final solution. Numerous typefaces were tested and presented, but none suited the client. At an additional meeting, the team showed a concept that used a classic sans serif treatment. As one team member recalls, "They went from wanting classical font to 'that's it!' fairly quickly." Out went the serifs. Similarly, the team worked through a series of realistic mountain images and moved toward a much smoother representative illustration. The final icon started life as the snowcap on one of the earlier renderings and was distilled through a dozen transformations.

The Result

After final selection, the exuberant client printed business cards, letterhead, and envelopes designed by TAK. Since then, the client has placed the new identity on company vehicles, trailers, signage, and its website.

Client: **Graphicwise**
Irvine, California, USA

Agency: **Graphicwise**
Irvine, California

The Challenge

Cutting-edge, simple, and *meaningful* are important adjectives to ascribe to a design studio's image if it wants to appeal to a wide variety of potential and existing clients. But Graphicwise also want to portray humor, imagination, and range to that same target market.

The Process

Being the client and the designer is always a challenge, but Graphicwise was up to the task. At first, the designers developed complex forms, caricatures, and intricate presentations. The process evolved into the distillation of a simple, light-hearted symbol that focused on building a character out of the letter *G*. A puzzle piece was added to the image, conveying the message that the studio can make a cohesive solution from numerous elements.

The Result

Both new and returning clients immediately got Graphicwise's message, which was employed on the studio's stationery program and website. The logo has garnered strong interest from numerous potential clients as well as existing clients since its launch.

The distillation of a simple, lighthearted symbol that focused on building a character out of the letter G serves as the focal point of Graphwise's delightful identity.

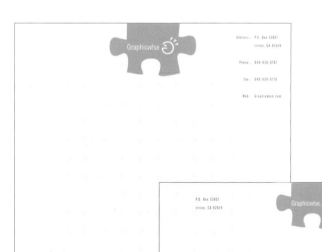

A puzzle piece was added to the equation in Graphicwise's identity program, applied to its letterhead and business cards, as shown here.

Client: **Richard Zeid Design**
Evanston, Illinois, USA

Agency: **Richard Zeid Design**
Evanston, Illinois

The Challenge

Objectivity is a designer's greatest virtue—a difficult professional stance to maintain when the client is you. When Richard Zeid created the identity for his studio, he found himself faced with a number of soul-searching questions. What does the concept say about me as a person? What does it say about me as a designer? What does it say about how I work and what I do? Does it convey what I do for my clients?

The Process

Because he had no client to set a schedule for delivery, Zeid took months to wade through the conceptual phase of the process, revisiting his work at various stages. He tested and retested each concept to see if it accurately portrayed his work methods and practices. In the end, he selected a dynamic graphic approach that focused on a modern, stylized *Z* letterform created with three shapes that symbolize his basic design process: research, design, and implementation. The visual was completed with the addition of a black sans serif type treatment and a bold orange and black color palette.

The Result

Given a client roster that includes the Chicago *Tribune*, the National Restaurant Association, Bank of America, and Edelman Public Relations, it's realistic to say that Zeid effectively and successfully conveyed his message to his target audence.

A dynamic graphic approach that focuses on a modern, stylized Z letterform, created with three shapes, symbolizes Richard Zeid's basic design process: research, design, and implementation.

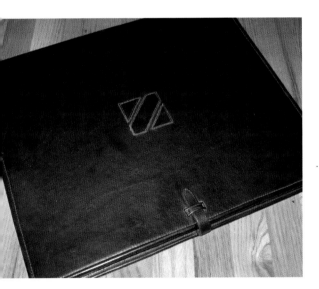

Zeid's stylized Z translates well when applied to promotional materials such as the studio's leather presentation binder.

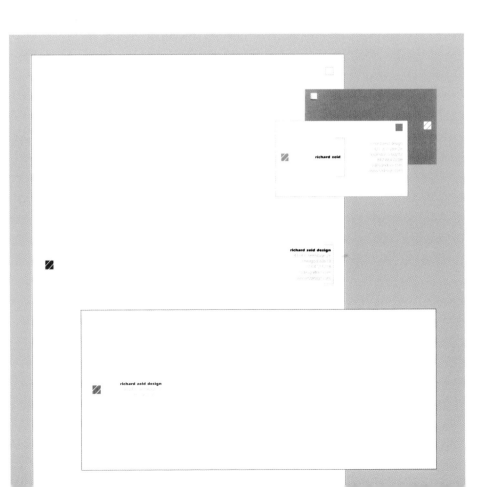

A strong black and orange palette communicates Zeid's commitment to dynamic design.

Client: **Staple Design**
New York, New York, USA

Agency: **Staple Design**
New York, New York; and Tokyo, Japan

The Challenge

With offices on New York's Lower East Side and in Tokyo, Staple Design is more than a design studio; it describes itself as a "shop/gallery/office /museum/record shop/bookstore/chair store/playground/romper room/design think tank/video game emporium/adult cinema." It goes without saying that the logo for this multi-faceted organization had to say a lot and convey an open-ended message at the same time. The real challenge, though, was that the studio itself had to define its own parameters and be its own client.

The Process

Numerous sketches and concept developments led to a dynamic typographic solution. The Staple Design team aimed for enough visual appeal to draw the attention of a youth-oriented audience but not enough to limit its usage on a variety of products and media. The result: A stark black, blue, orange, and white palette makes the raw calligraphic type treatment stand out against any background.

The Result

Thus far, the Staple Design logo has been applied to everything "except the kitchen sink." Besides its stationery program and website, the identity appears on the studio clothing line of casual wear, hats, key rings, lighters, belts, socks, pocketknives, T-shirts, and music CDs. The business has gained a strong and loyal following for its branded apparel and accessories as well as interest from retailers.

A "shop/gallery/office/muse-um/record shop/book-store/chair store/play-ground/romper room/design think tank/video game emporium/adult cinema" housed in the Reed Space in Manhattan's Lower East Side, Staple Design created a stark, calligraphic image to represent itself across a broad youth-oriented audi-ence in the United States and Japan.

Applied to the apparel and accessories it also designs and retails, the Staple Design logo appears even as custom embroidery and button branding on its line of jeans.

Client: **Hornall Anderson Design Works, Inc.**
Seattle, Washington, USA

Agency: **Hornall Anderson Design Works, Inc.**
Seattle, Washington

The Challenge

Designers are often their own worst clients. Besides dealing with self-expecta-
tions, the longevity of a design studio can—and often does—call for an occa-
sional logo redesign. After having invented its identity several times over the past
20 years, Hornall Anderson Design Works (HADW) decided it was time to attract
a new audience of potential clients and to alert existing ones that the studio's
designers remain fresh and current. The studio specifically wanted a new look
that would transition better from one that could potentially become dated.

The Process

The HADW design team directed its attention to a typographic solution that
incorporated a striking color palette. Playing with a variety of letterforms, the
team chose a witty yet uncomplicated solution. A capital *A* with the top chopped
off also forms the letter *H* viewed from an angled perspective. A rich. deep
orange and dark blue palette complements the treatment.

The new look and feel reflects a delightful way of connecting with existing clients
and potential new relationships; check-the-box options such as "laid back,"
"may save your life someday," and "stressed" are included in the stationery program, including the employees' business cards.

After 20 years of brand-building, Hornall Anderson Design Works refreshed its own identity, concentrating on a play on the letter A that also reads like the letter H seen at an angular perspective.

Hornall Anderson Design Works' new look and feel reflects the delightful way the company connects with its clients, by using check-the-box options such as "laid back," "may save your life someday," and "stressed" on its employees' business cards.

The Result

The new HADW identity has met with applause from the studio's existing and potential clients. Besides the stationery program, the HADW brand has been applied to signage and the website.

Client: **ThinkingCouch Interactive**
Singapore, Singapore

Agency: **ThinkingCouch Interactive**
Singapore, Singapore

ThinkingCouch Interactive

*The product of a brain-
storming session that took
place at an outdoor café,
ThinkingCouch's identity
expresses its belief that
the thinking process is the
most exciting and fun part
of design.*

The Challenge

When Thinkingcouch launched its studio, it wanted anyone and everyone to
understand its philosophy: that all good designs come about when clients and
designers effectively interact during the thinking process. The name and logo
were original ideas from a brainstorming session that took place at an outdoor
café. Ideas always emerge when one sits down, asks questions, and ponders
the possible solutions. To the members of ThinkingCouch, the thinking process
is the most exciting and fun part of design.

The Process

ThinkingCouch wanted its logo to convey that the studio is an "oasis of ideas."
After conceiving and developing a number of wayward modes of visually
expressing this, the images of a couch and a "thinking hat" got the most votes
from the team. They decided to combine the two elements. The most playful
solution incorporated the propeller from a child's beanie cap and a comfy, bright-
yellow couch. The final image was created using 3Dmax software and Adobe
Photoshop. Classic Garamond was used for the type treatment.

The Result

ThinkingCouch's logo has often been an icebreaker with new clients and a great
point of conversation with existing clients, who look forward to receiving the studio's many direct mail promotions.

*ThinkingCouch's sofa and
beanie propeller also grace
the opening page of its animated website.*

visible **theory**

Visible Theory's founder and creative director, Scott Wolfe, captured the studio's brand essence, using blue, red, white, and gray dots to form the significant letters of its name.

Client: **Visible Theory**
Pasadena, California, USA

Agency: **Visible Theory**
Pasadena, California

The Challenge

While every logo project presents its own unique challenges, designing an identity for your own company is especially difficult because of the closeness and attachment to the overall project. It is sometimes tough to distance yourself creatively.

The Process

Visible Theory's founder and creative director, Scott Wolfe, wanted to capture both typographically and metaphorically the essence of his brand's message: that Visible Theory delivers clear, consistent, and compelling design work. The final solution employs a series of blue, red, white, and gray dots that form the letters *V* and *T*, implying the studio can find a solution to any design equation with the simplicity and deft speed of an expert abacus user.

The Result

Visible Theory's crisp, eye-catching logo has been well received by both potential and existing clients, easily translating into all media including website, stationery program, and marketing materials.

visible theory

Delivering clear, consistent, and compelling design work for clients such as MGM, Sony Pictures, Twentieth-Century Fox, Columbia Tri-Star, and SkyMall Corporation, Visible Theory's logo implies the studio can find a solution to any design equation with the simplicity and deft speed of an expert abacus user.

UTOWA

Client: **UTOWA**
New York, New York, USA

Agency: **UTOWA**
New York, New York

The Challenge

The 1980s were a boomtime for extravagant and conspicuous consumption. In luxury branding as well as in fashion, '80s styles are seeing a resurgence. But creating an authentic '80s feel in a contemporary brand can be difficult—especially because the design tools and even the designers have so radically changed. For designer and entrepreneur Hiroshi Uemura, the biggest challenge was knowing when not to touch a design.

The Process

When Hiroshi Uemura developed the UTOWA store concept, he received a valuable asset from his father: the company's identity. Shu Uemura—also a designer—had created the UTOWA identity in the early '80s for a Japan-based beauty products company he was developing but never launched. The name had been amalgamated from Uemura, Tomen (a trading company), and Kiowa (a traditional medicine producer). The brand was mothballed—completely unused, but not forgotten—until Hiroshi approached his father with his new UTOWA store/design studio/event space concept. Both his uncanny design-trend sense and his desire to pay tribute to his father's work kept Hiroshi from altering the design. Instead, he adapted the store design and all of the store's imagery to the logo.

The Result

Although it is thoroughly contemporary, even cutting edge, the UTOWA logo speaks of luxury in a visual language untainted by the economic upheavals of the late '80s and the '90s. Initial consumer reaction has been strong. The store surpassed its sales estimates, its design studio is extremely busy, and bookings have been solid for its event space for the first six months of business since it opened in 2003.

A new concept in cutting-edge design and retail, UTOWA merges a retail store, creative agency, café, art gallery, and event space—all connected by a common typographic brand and a common message of luxurious aesthetic.

UTOWA's main space houses flowers, beauty products, clothes, and trendy electronics side by side as well as an area that can be rapidly converted for catered events.

Client: **Mark McLaughlin**
San Diego, California, USA

Agency: **Mark McLaughlin**
San Diego, California

The Challenge

Perhaps the toughest challenge in self-branding is the lack of deadline. It's all too easy to run overtime or set the design aside in favor of other projects. Next to that, the designer's biggest dilemma is coming up with an identity that will speak of design to diverse clients. In Mark McLaughlin's own words, "I didn't want to categorize myself into one particular style. I wanted a logo that could appeal to a wide range of audiences, but also communicate my range of capabilities. I was determined to create a logo that could reinforce my initials, *MM*."

The Process

McLaughlin began experimenting with different shapes and colors. As he said, "I wanted to break away from the typical typography and bring another element into my initials. I settled on the idea of connecting arrows into the letter *M*. I continued to design different version of this arrowed *M* and discovered an interesting method of breaking the letter into two separate arrows, each moving in a different direction. These multidirectional arrows represent the different capabilities I provide and versatility of my skills. In addition, the two elements of the logo reinforce my double *M* initials."

The Result

McLaughlin attributes over half the identity projects he has received directly to this logo. "I want a logo like yours" is a common phrase he hears from prospective clients. The bottom line? McLaughlin's profits have tripled since inception of this logo.

Mark McLaughlin's logo addresses a diverse list of existing and prospective clients and his own versatility, employing his initials MM and multidirectional arrows.

ANA MARTINS

After vetting dozens of ideas from designers as well as friends and relatives, Ana Martins's brand identity was the result of soul-searching and a vague feeling her dream of an ideal identity was impossible—until she realized she already had the solution and just needed a designer to bring it to fruition.

Client: **Ana Martins Public Relations**
New York, New York, USA

Agency: **Inoviz**
New York, New York

The Challenge

Ana Martins took a sabbatical from her New York–based public relations business after the September 11 tragedy to return to her native Portugal to spend time with her family. While there, she began work on a new brand mark for her company. After vetting dozens of ideas from designers as well as friends and relatives, Martins returned to New York with a firm idea of what she didn't want and a vague feeling that her heart's desire was impossible.

As many of her clients are in couture fashion, she wanted a logo in nude tones accented with a copper metallic palette. It needed to be edgy and modern as well as abstract and classic. It needed to be brief but with impact, and it needed to make an entrance. Without a lot of hope, she approached a favorite designer, Marco Gonsalvez, then brought his work to Inoviz to be finalized.

The Process

What Martins didn't realize was that her string of abortive attempts had been highly productive. Unlike many design clients, she arrived at the designer having tried her hand at creating the logo and had already seen enough bad designs that she was mentally prepared to appreciate a good one, even if it jumped effortlessly off the designer's sketch pad on the first try. And it did—after a single 15-minute conversation. As she put it, "Once the first sketch was done we couldn't even look at anything else." With a structure in front of them, the Inoviz team was able to bring the logo to life by selecting and setting the type, finishing the palette, and retouching the icon.

The Result

Ana Martins loves the logo, as do her clients. As a public relations specialist, Martins appreciates the importance of consistent branding and makes sure that her logo appears wherever possible.

The designer's vision of an "Allentown Proud" identity emerged while sitting in a traffic jam with a sketchbook and plenty of time right after a meeting with the client.

Client: **Greater Lehigh Valley Chamber of Commerce**
Lehigh Valley, Pennsylvania, USA

Agency: **Zurek Design**
Easton, Pennsylvania

The Challenge

What's the first thing that comes to mind when you hear the word Allentown? Admit it; it's the Billy Joel song by the same name, right? In truth, Allentown, Pennsylvania, is a vibrant, growing city with devoted citizens who have invested in downtown businesses and supported the city through up years and down years.

The Lehigh Valley Chamber of Commerce wanted to create a campaign and logo that would represent the pride the locals feel for their city. The department approached Zurek Design with a slogan in place—"Allentown Proud"—and no budget. Pamela Zurek's challenge was to create a logo that could be reproduced in a variety of formats, both large and tiny.

The Process

As Zurek recalls, "After meeting with the Greater Lehigh Valley Chamber of Commerce, I realized I needed to come up with an image that reflected the dynamic downtown community. I was thinking about it on the drive back from Allentown to my office in Easton. Traffic on Route 22 was backed up to a standstill. I jotted down the image of a heart nested inside the *o* in Allentown and used a mix of upper- and lowercase letters to give a friendly feeling to the words. Back in my office, I came up with four or five alternate ideas, but the committee chose the one I came up with in the traffic jam. It's probably the best thing ever to come out of a Route 22 traffic tie-up!"

The Result

Zurek's top-of-mind sketch has been refined and applied to stickers and decals that have been plastered all over the city. The Chamber of Commerce has freely shared the logo with downtown business owners, who have used it on stationery, shopping bags, and promotional material. It's also been used on the Allentown website and newsletter.

"The result for me has been very gratifying. The logo is slowly becoming recognized throughout the Lehigh Valley area and is always a highlight of my portfolio presentations to new clients. Although I took the project on a pro bono basis and wasn't compensated for my work, the process was enjoyable, and the payoff in PR made it all worth it!" Zurek concludes.

Turner Creative
marketing communications

Creativity and fun are expressed in this identity for a marketing communications and copywriting agency that wanted an image that steered far from trite visual solutions.

Client: **Turner Creative**
Mill Valley, California, USA

Agency: **Project6 Design**
Berkeley, California

The Challenge

Abstract concepts pose numerous challenges for the designer. Because there's no concrete object or landscape or activity from which a tangible visual can be derived, abstracts such as data analysis and investment banking fall prey to subjective interpretation as opposed to the objective transmission of an intended message. A marketing communications and copywriting agency based in Marin County, California, Turner Creative needed a visual point of difference that clearly explained its abstract products and steered far from trite visual solutions.

The Process

Hired to craft this difficult image, Project6 Design explored typographic solutions until the team landed on a Bodoni type treatment. But the typography on its own it was too classic. The team coupled a visual message of creativity and fun by adding bubbles that rise above the dot of the name's lowercase letter *i*. As one team member explained, "The combination of classic typeface and bubbly orange circles creates an unusual mix that just puts a smile on your face."

The Result

The lively, open appearance of Turner Creative's identity communicates with clarity and impact a solid visual message that the company delivers creative talent and strategic communications solutions.

Turner Creative's bubbly orange circles and lively human images strike a unique chord on its website.

Turner Creative
marketing communications

find your voice

Imagine how powerful your marketing could be if all your communications spoke with a single, clear voice.

Turner Creative gives your company that critical advantage. We provide the creative talent and strategic expertise companies need to communicate with clarity and impact.

From websites and brochures to direct mail and advertising, we develop the marketing tools that establish your brand, distinguish your product and inspire your customers to act.

▪▪lasalle
COMMUNICATIONS

■lasalle
COMMUNICATIONS
LaSalle Communications
111B Bromfield Terrace
Manchester, MO 63021

Marketing and public relations are the building blocks that lead to successful communication between a business and its client roster. These same activities lead to solid and steady business growth, as portrayed in LaSalle Communications' identity.

Client: **LaSalle Communications**
Manchester, Missouri, USA

Agency: **CFX Creative**
Vancouver, British Columbia, Canada

The Challenge
Based in Manchester, Missouri, LaSalle Communications offers mid-size businesses and consultancies a variety of marketing services including media planning, eBusiness consulting, corporate communications, eMarketing, and market research. LaSalle's public relations practice covers the range from business-to-business communications and employee and media relations to product and program publicity. To portray the abstract concepts that are the core of LaSalle's business, its founder, Kim LaSalle, tasked CFX Creative to develop an identity with visual "legs."

The Process
Marketing and public relations are the building blocks that not only lead to successful communication between a business and its client roster but also are stepping stones to solid and steady business growth. CFX Creative visualized this strong message, using three small squares to form the letter *L*. The icon is supported by a bold and direct type treatment of the company name.

The Result
LaSalle Communications' entire identity package bears this dynamic identity, from its website and HTML newsletter to business cards, letterhead, envelopes, and other business forms. A ghosted three-dimensional version of the icon was employed on printed identity materials to further convey LaSalle's three-dimensional approach to communications.

File   Edit   View   Go   Favorites

OVERVIEW   EXPERTISE   CONTACT US

■lasalle
COMMUNICATIONS

OVERVIEW
News & Articles
Leadership
How We Work
Case Studies

OVERVIEW

LaSalle Communications is a full service marketing agency for progressive companies like yours. We deliver innovative thinking and results-driven strategies for out-smarting, out-selling, and out-styling your competition.

As a strategic partner in your business, we understand:

■ Where you've been and where you want to go.

■ How you influence stakeholders.

■ How you think and how you see things.

■ How you make decisions and how you give direction.

■ How you deal with conflict and how you deal with change.

■ What wakes you up at 2 a.m.

■ Who keeps you looking over your shoulder.

We help you expect the unexpected in your drive for success. Applying insight, imagination, inspiration (and, often, perspiration), we know what makes you distinguished and what makes you distinguishing.

LaSalle Communications' strong color palette and building block iconography is expanded on in the company's website.

Client: **CFX Creative**
Vancouver, British Columbia, Canada

Agency: **CFX Creative**
Vancouver, British Columbia, Canada

The Challenge

Vancouver-based studio CFX Creative, headed by founder and CEO Carly H. Franklin, specializes in graphic design, corporate identity, and Web development. The challenge the studio faced in designing its own mark was how to give equitable billing to all three services and make a strong statement about how the services are rendered.

The Process

Creating a mark that offered clues to services was simple enough. But the revelation that one wordmark candidate was actually a play on words—"see effects"—made the final name selection a breeze. The design team then experimented with an abstract rendering of an eye to sublimate a message that the studio's work is engaging and eye-catching. A clear blue color scheme sends supporting messages of clarity, optimism, and flow.

The Result

CFX Creative's icon and wordmark have been flexible enough to seamlessly evolve from the website's initial launch to its current use in marketing and promotional initiatives.

An abstract eye that sees effects serves as CFX Creative's iconographic message.

CFX Creative's supporting messages of clarity, optimism, and flow ring true through its crystal-blue color scheme and eye-catching visuals, seen here on its letterhead and website.

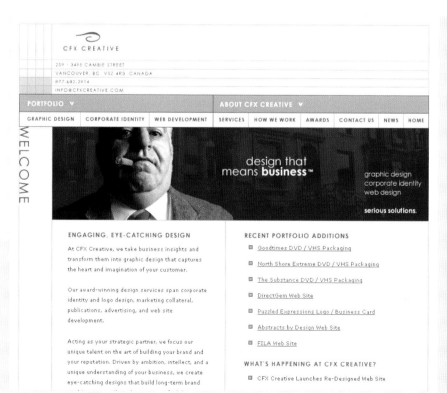

Promoting a study on the health of the design industry can be a challenge, which CFX Creative faced when it collaborated on the Industry Snapshot identity with Core 77 Design Network, a Web-based community for design enthusiasts seeking trends, information, resources, and opportunities, and marketing specialist LaSalle Communications.

Client: **Industry Snapshot**
Vancouver, British Columbia, Canada

Agency: **CFX Creative**
Vancouver, British Columbia, Canada

The Challenge

The design industry is, in many ways, organic. The design process develops gradually and naturally. The visual result derived from this process forms a basic and inherent part of something else—a business, a product, a service. The fact that humans are involved from inception to completion makes design itself organic. The continued growth of the design industry even requires the study of humans and their relationship to demographics, business practices, and growth strategies.

CFX Creative partnered with Core 77 Design Network, a Web-based community for design enthusiasts seeking trends, information, resources, and opportunities, and marketing specialist LaSalle Communications to conduct a primary research study that analyzed how the fittest design professionals are surviving in an unfit economic environment. The group's findings were coordinated into a presentation entitled "Industry Snapshot." The challenges lay in visualizing the human aspects of design and the contemporaneous nature of the study while appealing to a broad range of people with definitive tastes and styles.

The Process

CFX Creative chose a simple geometric shape to represent study participants. The team found the identity in a type treatment with a square, industrial shape and feel, visually conveying the name of the study and representing the design industry as a whole. A deep earth-toned palette added solidity to the overall message.

The Result

Industry Snapshot's mark was employed on Core 77's website and figured prominently on the cover page of the study results, which were distributed to participants in PDF format. The presentation and its brand were so well accepted by the design community that CFX Creative, The Core 77 Design Network, and LaSalle Communications took it upon themselves to conduct a similar study in 2003 for presentation in 2004.

**INDUSTRY SNAPSHOT
SEPTEMBER 2002**

A PRIMARY RESEARCH STUDY COVERING
DEMOGRAPHICS, BUSINESS CHARACTERISTICS,
GROWTH STRATEGIES, AND BEST PRACTICES
WITHIN THE DESIGN INDUSTRY.

CORE 77   CFX CREATIVE

The human side of design looms largely in Industry Snapshot's identity, which appears on PDF-formatted study results and a website that presents the results virtually to people who couldn't attend the actual presentation.

An abstract rendition of
a paper plane serves as
the icon for Pointe Aviation's
fleet of single-engine
airplanes.

Client: **Pointe Aviation**
Carlsbad, California, USA

Agency: **Graphicwise**
Irvine, California

The Challenge
Pointe Aviation owns and operates a fleet of single-engine airplanes that trans-
port passengers throughout southwestern California. Instant brand recognition is
an essential element in the air travel business. Go to any airport and look at the
array of type treatments and symbols employed by both large and small airlines
in an effort to catch viewers' eyes on the ground and in the air.

The company knew it needed a cutting-edge design that was simple and to the
point as well as legible at a distance and on printed materials. No other direction
was given to the contracted design studio, Graphicwise.

The Process
Brainstorming and over two dozen sketches yielded the final Pointe Aviation
identity. A clean type treatment with a slight 1930s modern flavor was paired
with the simple graphic shape of a paper airplane ascending to the sky.

The Result
Graphicwise's finished design was unveiled before the entire staff and management of Pointe Aviation, which overwhelmingly approved. The mark was implemented on building signage, the stationery program, employee polo shirts, and
on the company's fleet of aircraft.

A dynamic stream of
motion is presented in
Pointe Aviation's letterhead,
which highlights the logo
pinpoint trajectory.

Pointe Aviation's logo is
portrayed in both positive
and negative space on its
business cards.

TravelPORT
A CENDANT COMPANY

The consolidated image and clear positioning statement of Travelport addresses the company's leading end-to-end corporate travel solution, providing online booking, GDS, fulfillment solutions, data and profile management, service, and support.

Client: **Travelport**
Seattle, Washington, USA

Agency: **Hornall Anderson Design Works, Inc**
Seattle, Washington

The Challenge

The corporate travel industry is densely populated with subsidiaries of such high-powered companies as Microsoft and Nike. Formerly known as Highwire, Travelport, a Cendant Company division, commissioned Hornall Anderson Design Works (HADW) in 2003 to create a consolidated image and a clear positioning statement as the leading end-to-end corporate travel solution, providing online booking, GDS (global distribution systems), fulfillment solutions, data and profile management, service, and support.

The Process

Travelport's makeover began with a complete rebranding strategy that built the new identity from the ground up and clearly portrayed the company's limitless capabilities and opportunities for expansion. The HADW design team's solution incorporated photographic images that portrayed travel themes from flight to trains to buses. A bright, bold palette was employed to capture the users' attention and pull them into the experience of the promotional program.

The Result

HADW's new identity, reminiscent of many American airport wayfinding systems, has given Travelport an appropriate yet distinct feel that sets it apart from the competition.

The back of Travelport's business cards present the time zones of the world's major cities as well as its Seattle home base.

Promotional coupons issued at trade shows offer readers a glimpse of the world covered by Travelport as well as strong branding for the company's refreshed identity.

General Motors wanted to elevate its stature with an upmarket appearance attracting consumers to its family of brands, including Chevrolet, Pontiac, Cadillac, Buick, GMC, Saturn, Hummer, and Saab. FutureBrand's solution looks like a badge that's applied to the coporation's line of vehicles.

General Motors' refreshed identity was used to promote the company's 75th anniversary in the automotive business, which was heralded in collateral materials and displays and on its website.

The new General Motors logo was employed in ad campaigns promoting the company's latest line of vehicles.

Client: **General Motors Corporation**
Detroit, Michigan, USA

Agency: **FutureBrand**
New York, New York, USA

The Challenge

Creating a new brand can be much easier than repositioning a familiar identity that has deeply invested equity. The FutureBrand team discovered this truth when commissioned to refresh General Motors' logo. The automotive industry relies heavily on consumer recognition of its brands, which convey such perceived expectations as status, reliability, speed, coolness, and adventure. General Motors wanted to elevate its stature with an upmarket appearance attracting consumers to its family of brands, including Chevrolet, Pontiac, Cadillac, Buick, GMC, Saturn, Hummer, and Saab. Because the identity needed to brand onto print, broadcast, Web, signage, and the vehicles themselves, it was decided that a three-dimensional insignia would have the greatest impact.

The Process

After careful review of the brand's existing equities, FutureBrand chose to develop a mark that looked like the badge that's actually applied to the vehicles. The team explored a number of interpretations that presented the mark in different finishes, colors, and presentations of the three-dimensional appearance. In the end, a blue reflective version was selected because it retains past associations with General Motors' blue corporate color and the GM logotype. The graphic reflection that appears in the final rendition of the background suggests the profile of a vehicle.

The Result

Initially, FutureBrand's new brand identity was employed in the company's corporate advertising initiatives and website, www.gm.com. This application has since been expanded into other high-end, high-profile applications including PowerPoint presentations, select print literature, select facility signage, and promotional initiatives such as auto shows and product rollout events. While the three-dimensional GM brand was intended as an alternative to the historic two-dimensional brand mark, it has gained widespread acceptance and preference throughout General Motors Corporation.

A company that specializes in ship turbocharger engineering and maintenance, Scan Turbo's identity crosses multiple cultures in an industry that's known for a lack of branding and identity design.

Client: **Scan Turbo**
Bremerhaven, Germany

Agency: **Braue: Branding & Corporate Design**
Bremerhaven, Germany

The Challenge

Scan Turbo, of Bremerhaven, Germany, specializes in ship turbocharger engineering and maintenance. With customers all over Europe, overseas and—literally—on the seas, the company's brand crosses multiple cultures in an industry that's known for a lack of branding and identity design. Braue's challenge was to visualize the speed and dynamic of Scan Turbo's core competency and bring it up out of the crowd without distancing it from its clients.

The Process

First, Braue defined what turbo engineering is about: technology at the highest level and the power of turbo engines. This became the team's visual goal. Then they began scouting to see if others had succeeded in visually defining the concept. Their research online and in special-interest magazines and trade publications revealed a predominance of 1980s-style identities. The Braue team eschewed this industry trend, studying instead major German technology companies like Siemens. Here, they found designs that reflected the present and future of turbo engineering rather than its past.

The Result

Scan Turbo's corporate redesign was extremely well received by its clients and within the industry. The client loves the new corporate look, as it represents the company's growth in recent years. Braue incorporated abstract visuals of speed and flow on printed materials to further reinforce the brand's core message. The website cleverly incorporates a turbo stream sound element in the design.

Scan Turbo's business cards reflect the personas employed by German technology companies rather than the 1980s-style imagery used by the rest of the turbo industry.

The future of turbo engineering, strength, and energy are the messages addressed throughout Scan Turbo's identity program.

Air France's On Air service promises young, style-conscious, high-end passengers luxurious comfort during flight without conflicting with or overpowering the Air France brand.

Client: **Air France**
Paris, France

Agency: **Desgrippes Gobé Group**
New York, New York, USA

The Challenge

Air France is a well-documented pioneer and leader in the global travel industry. One of only two airlines to commission and fly passengers across the Atlantic aboard the supersonic Concorde, Air France was the first Western carrier to offer regular flights to Beijing, China, in the 1960s. The airline was also the first to offer nonsmoking flights.

The airline planned the year-and-a-half-long launch of its new On Air service, which features l'Espace Premiere and l'Espace Affaires cabins and lounges—the ultimate in comfort and design. The rollout program included presentations to a worldwide network of hotel partners and consumers.

One of the airline's main objectives was to develop a strong visual subbrand that would not overpower the existing Air France identity but would still speak to a younger, style-conscious, high-end target audience.

The Process

The Desgrippes Gobé Group design team developed an emotion-driven design strategy that defined the visceral attributes necessary to connect the passenger to the program: sleek, modern, stylish, comfortable, and elegant. The focal point is an iconic line drawing of a modern seat promising luxurious comfort during flight. Air France's signature red is coupled with a distinctive warm gray that complements the airline's blue, white, and red color scheme.

The Result

Due for launch in the summer of 2004, On Air's mark has received many kudos from Air France executives and focus groups.

The fluid lines of the On Air identity are branded on amenities such as Air France's pillows, blankets, promotional items, and dinnerware.

Client:	**Sky Team**
	Paris, France
Agency:	**Desgrippes Gobé Group**
	New York, New York, USA

The Challenge

Too many cooks are apt spoil the broth. So, when a single brand identity needs to encompass the core messages and desires of six member airlines, it takes the objective eye of a well-seasoned design team to maintain the integrity of the finished product. SkyTeam is a global alliance of airlines including Air France, Czech Airlines, AeroMexico, Alitalia, Korean Air, and Delta Airlines. The partnership offers frequent business travelers access to a network of 500 destinations in 110 countries via 7,865 daily flights. Besides ease in making guaranteed reservations and connections, SkyTeam also offers service enhancements such as increased access to airport lounges and priority check-in.

The Process

To satisfy all of the partners' ideas and core messages, the Desgrippes Gobé design team developed a logo based on three central ideas: universality, distinctiveness, and shared values. The ribbon motif is a universal designation of quality and sophistication. The team employed a stylized version of this element that implies luxury spanning the world. The elegant shape of the central icon and supporting type treatment conveys an air of elegance and distinctiveness. The tagline "Caring more about you" reinforces SkyTeam's commitment to instill trust in its patrons and to provide the highest-quality service.

The Result

The carefully conceived new brand has received major exposure and positive commentary since it appeared in a series of television spots.

A global alliance of airlines including Air France, Czech Airlines, AeroMexico, Alitalia, Korean Air, and Delta Airlines, SkyTeam's identity expresses the harmony and luxury service the partnership offers frequent business travelers.

SkyTeam's elegant logo brands promotional items used in the upscale airline lounges such as the ones pictured here.

To reach their audience, the Frontline team invented Mister Van Dyke. A mid-twentieth-century advertising persona, he quickly became the logo's key visual.

Client: **Frontline, GmbH**
Münster, Germany

Agency: **H2D2, Office for Visual Communication**
Frankfurt, Germany

The Challenge

The current youth market is visually jaded. The target of innumerable products and services as well as visual competition from print, broadcast, Web, and video, this audience has an expendable income that far exceeds that of previous generations. But just like earlier youth market groups, the current generation needs to identify with the products and services it purchases. Each consumer must feel that he or she is making a wholly personal statement with each purchase. Van Dyke is a new StreetFashion brand created by Frontline and geared to consumers ages 18 to 30. The H2D2 design team was contracted to develop an identity that would resonate with this highly demanding target group.

The Process

The H2D2 team took two different routes before achieving the desired visual result. *Van Dyke* is a Dutch surname. The word *van* means "from" and was a familiar mark of noble lineage for many centuries in the Netherlands. The team initially developed a modernized coat of arms with a heraldry that evoked a traditional appearance, but the result didn't resonate with the intended audience when tested. The team then chose to invent a fictional person. Mister Van Dyke, a mid-twentieth-century advertising persona, became the logo's key visual. A solid and contemporary black and earth-tone palette was selected to reinforce the stylistic simplicity the target youth market enjoys.

The Result

The van Dyke logo was applied to textile patterns, labeling, advertising, and promotional materials, including shopping bags and hang tags. Although there was limited time to produce the completed brand, the client was absolutely convinced and enthusiastic about the final design solution. The van Dyke brand will come to market in early 2004.

Beyond its use to brand packaging, the Mister Van Dyke logo demonstrates intrinsic and extrinsic value of its own when used as a printed clothing pattern.

Client:

Blue Q
Pittsfield, Massachusetts, USA

Agency:

Modern Dog Design Company
Seattle, Washington, USA

The Challenge

In the $90 billion beauty products market, many brands stand out for their purity, natural ingredients, and promises of luxurious experiences. One stands out for its wry humor, reminiscent of *Cracked* magazine's product parodies. If a sense of humor is, as author Edward de Bono claims, "the highest form of intelligence," then Blue Q must be the smartest company in the beauty business. Blue Q produces a line of high-quality bath and body products in edgy, humorous packaging, with names like Wash Away Your Sins, Miso Pretty, Virgin/Slut, Dirty Girl, Total Bitch, and Tainted Love.

Modern Dog had previously worked on Voodoo, Bubble Monkey, and Mr. Pit Stop. In the current line, they also designed Who Da Man? and Mother Theresa. Now, Modern Dog had to fit identities for Mofo and Mullet into this unique line.

The Process

For the Mullet brand, Blue Q wanted a visual cross between a 1970s shampoo bottle and a car cleaner/wax logo. Modern Dog's design team studied shampoo bottles and advertising from the 1970s, then began sketching. A long-term personal desire to poke fun at commercial packaging spurred them on, and they just continued sketching until they hit the ideal design.

The primary influence on Mofo was the 1970s *Superfly* movie poster and album cover typography. The design team assessed and improved the brand's street credibility by studying hip-hop culture and graffiti. In the process, they generated all of the packaging copy, which felt like a natural extension of creating the logo.

The Result

Mitch Nash, cofounder of Blue Q, says Modern Dog is continually "dumbing down" the company's products—high praise under the circumstances. The Mullet logo has been used on soap packaging, postcards, and website icons. It also appears on products including shampoo, body/car wash, and lip balm. Nash adds, "We just came back from Mexico City and saw the products there too. So the logo has worked cross-culturally."

To create the Mullet logo and packaging, the Modern Dog team studied 1970s-era advertising and shampoo bottles—then set out to lampoon them.

Modern hip-hop art and graffiti were melded with 1970s art—particularly the Superfly posters and album cover—to create the distinctive Mofo brand.

Client: **Burton Snowboards**
Burlington, Vermont, USA

Agency: **Staple Design**
New York, New York, USA; and Tokyo, Japan

The Challenge

Snowboarding may seem like a recent phenomenon, but the Vermont-based Burton Snowboards—the first major snowboard manufacturer—has been around since 1977, when Jake Burton Carpenter started it on a shoestring. Carpenter himself championed the sport, gaining access for snowboarding runs in ski areas and even setting up the first competitions (he's still considered the company's most avid product tester). By the mid-1990s, the company had worldwide operations, and at the 2002 Winter Olympics in Salt Lake City, three Burton pro boarders won medals.

When Burton extended its line to include a new proprietary, branded performance wear line called Burton AK Continuum, it commissioned Staple Design to create both the visual identity and apparel.

The Process

Staple Design had two advantages coming in: They already had a long working relationship with Burton, and team members are serious snowboard enthusiasts in their own right. They knew what visuals would resonate with this growing target market. They considered the end user, the feel of snowboarding down a pipe, and the emotions inspired by the word continuum. The graphic symbol conveys the feel of continuous motion into infinity, while the square sans serif type treatment structurally supports the image.

The Result

The highest level of the company's performance gear, strong sales of the AK Continuum line are the best testament to the power of its visual identity. The brand has received major applause and garnered major sales since its launch in 2003.

The Staple Design team captured the exhilaration of snowboarding down a pipe and the feel of continuous motion into infinity, using square sans serif type to structurally support the image.

The F in Fundamental's iconic identity represents the band's name, while the arrows symbolize its music's signature percussive beat. The type is chopped and mixed to characterize the variety of music the band plays.

Client: **Fundamental**
Bend, Oregon, USA

Agency: **Panagrafik**
Bend, Oregon

The Challenge

Creatives can often be more difficult clients than corporations. Strong and differing opinions can make the job of brand design exceptionally challenging.

Musicians are no different than other creatives in this respect. Fundamental is an Oregon-based band that plays a blend of punk, phunk, groove, and rock and roll. When the band decided it needed a visual brand, each member had a different concept in mind. Before matters got out of hand, they called on Panagrafik to develop a solution.

Fundamental went to the studio with a few sketches of what they thought they wanted. Luckily, Panagrafik design team members were already fans of the band and its music. They knew Fundamental's style.

The Process

Panagrafik presented three concepts that looked nothing like the sketches the band had brought in with them. Two of those ideas were fused to create the finished identity: The letter *F* represents Fundamental's name, and the down-pointed arrows symbolize the bass beat that gets the band's fans going during a performance. The typographic treatment is chopped and mixed like the variety of music the band plays.

The Result

Implemented on the band's promotional materials and demo CD labels, the new identity ushered in a transition. This clean brand image has been well received by fans and attracted the interest of sponsors. What's more, Fundamental is now in talks with several record labels, with their first full-length album due to launch in the near future.

Fundamental fans themselves, the Panagrafik design team implemented the new identity on promotional materials and demo CD labels. These have been so well received that the band has attracted the interest of sponsors and record label executives.

Even Fundamental's drum kit is branded with the new identity, reinforcing it with fans and clubgoers while they're on the stage.

Staple Design took a democratic approach to the design of the documentary Deadstock's identity, posting a selection of alternative logos on a website and asking viewers—members of their target audience—to vote.

Client: ***Deadstock* (Documentary)**
New York, New York, USA

Agency: **Staple Design**
New York, New York; and Tokyo, Japan

The Challenge

Regardless if it's a blockbuster, art, or an indie production, every motion picture has an identity that appears long before the opening title hits the screen. *Deadstock* was no different. The producers of this film about a subculture that's passionate about sneakers came to Staple Design to develop an identity that would appear on numerous media.

The Process

The Staple Design team took a democratic approach to the development of the logo. After creating a number of concepts, they posted the collection on a website and asked online viewers to cast their ballot for their favorite. A lowercase type treatment enclosed in double quotes executed in a simple typewriter face superimposed over a dynamic photograph of legs and sneaker-clad feet won the majority vote.

The Result

From collateral materials, promotional items, print ads, T-shirts and other clothing items, plus the opening title, the *Deadstock* logo is set to appear during the investor-relations stage in 2004 and preproduction through postproduction and first release in 2005.

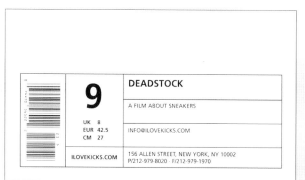

A dynamic photo of legs and sneaker-clad feet in motion adds visual support to this identity for a film about a subculture that's passionate about sneakers.

T-shirts printed with the Deadstock documentary's logo help brand the film in the eyes of potential investors. During production, the T-shirts will be worn by the film crew, and when it's released, these same shirts will serve as promotional items.

textureline.

Client: **L'Oréal**
Paris, France

Agency: **Bergman Associates**
New York, New York, USA

The Challenge

Acquired by L'Oréal, ARTec produces lines of hair care products that are exclusively sold in salons nationwide. ARTec's point-of-difference is its use of natural ingredients such as kiwi fruit extract, juniper, angelica, and tea tree oil in its formulations. Appealing to a cosmopolitan audience who demand products that don't contain harsh chemicals, but do promise impressive styling results, the company called on Bergman Associates to develop branding and packaging that would promise style, quality, and natural ingredients to an upscale, young audience.

The Process

Years of experience in the beauty and cosmetic industries made it easy for the Bergman Associates design team to identify key visual aspects that would appeal to this discerning, style-conscious market, who are willing to spend more for exclusive salon-only products to maintain their hair. The team developed a striking sans serif identity that stands apart from the competition: the identity is placed perpendicularly on bottles and packaging.

The Result

When they were launched in the early 2000s, Textureline shampoos, conditioners, and styling products gave competitors, such as Aveda, a run for their market share. Bergman Associates' logo for the brand continues to keep it top of mind and on the top of salon shelves.

Appealing to a young audience of style-conscious consumers who prefer products that contain natural ingredients, Textureline speaks directly to both male and female viewers with a strong type treatment and sleek packaging.

Rather than using visual vehicles such as flowers or plants to convey Textureline's nature-based formulation, Bergman Associates addressed the product line's ability to deliver sophistication and style as its strongest selling point.

Client: **Candy Station**
Bremerhaven, Germany

Agency: **Braue: Branding & Corporate Design**
Bremerhaven, Germany

The Challenge

Image means everything in the music business. Regardless of style, the visual representation of a band or a performer speaks thousands of words before the first note is played. A new player in the recording industry, Candy Station wanted a brand identity that would stand out against its peers in this highly competitive world. The company called on Braue to create a cheerful brand that presented its point of difference up front.

The Process

The Braue design team studied consumer and trade music magazines and surfed numerous websites in its early design exploration. Research and intensive exploration yielded a friendly, playful, likable gathering of retro graphic elements and colors that also possessed a tongue-in-cheek attitude. The image was tested on a number of models, including a Rolodex-style business card. The team went to the music world's largest industry fair, Musikmesse Frankfurt, to test the concept for originality and accessibility. The response was unanimous: The logo and business card were unofficially awarded "most interesting and unique design."

The Result

Besides receiving positive feedback from conventiongoers in the test stage, Candy Station's identity and sound have attracted a strong following among DJs and music collectors.

To create a strong contrast to their client's music industry competition, Braue used lighthearted retro graphics to create a point of difference for this urban music label, conveying a positive and cheerful tongue-in-cheek message.

Candy Station's identity appears not only on CDs but also on promotional materials and T-shirts that help the music label reach its youthful, trend-aware audience.

The Rolodex-shaped business cards accentuate the retro feel of Candy Station's logo. Tested at the world's largest music fair, the cards were enthusiastically received by attendees because of their originality and strong appeal.

The GenoKids logo draws from cartoons, comics, childrens' cereal boxes, and toys—a broad cross-section of the target audience's favorite visuals.

Client: **Volksbank eG Bremerhaven-Wesermünde**
Bremerhaven, Germany

Agency: **Braue: Branding & Corporate Design**
Bremerhaven, Germany

The Challenge

Bankers around the world know that educating modern-day youngsters about the value of saving money is not as simple as giving away toy banks. Marketing programs need to include stronger incentives, including an identity that catches youthful eyes as quickly as a favorite cartoon and holds their attention longer than the latest video game. When Braue: Branding & Corporate Design was asked to develop a visual identity for GenoKids, a new youth banking program, it faced an additional challenge: to include the corporate color palette of one of Germany's largest banks, Volksbank eG Bremerhaven-Wesermünde. The logo also had to resemble the identity used to promote the bank's previous youth club promotion, GenoClub.

The Process

The Braue design team interviewed six- to ten-year-olds in kindergartens and schools to get a better understanding of what they like and dislike. The team also explored toy stores, watched loads of TV cartoons, played videogames, and read comic books to get into the head of the average German child. Their designs reflect this dedicated approach. The orange swirl, crown, and accompanying cartoon character children are reminiscent of Pokémon and a host of other current youth icons.

The Result

The client was overwhelmed by the success of this initiative, which saw the opening of numerous new accounts by parents for their kids, a requirement for joining the club. Children's participation in the club's activities also increased nearly 500 percent.

Bright color palettes, cartoon characters, and vibrant fonts amplify the GenoKids logo on the Web and on printed matter.

The refreshed EMS brand (above), created by Desgrippes Gobé, captures the "gotta get out" attitude of its loyal customer base of hardcore mountain climbers and its new audience of young travel and mountain sports enthusiasts. The icon depicts a road up a high mountain toward a bright sun while maintaining the integrity and feel of the original mark (below).

Client: **Eastern Mountain Sports**
Peterborough, New Hampshire, USA

Agency: **Desgrippes Gobé Group**
New York, New York, USA

The Challenge

A leading manufacturer and retailer of outdoor gear and apparel, Eastern Mountain Sports (EMS) wanted to created a branding program that would achieve three goals. The company wanted to update its existing logo. It wanted to appeal to a younger, broader customer base interested in travel and mountain sports such as climbing, cross-country skiing, camping, snowshoeing, canoeing, cycling, kayaking, and hiking. The company also wanted to send a message to its loyal consumer base of hardcore climbers that EMS still stands for knowledge and knowhow.

The Process

The Desgrippes Gobé design team explored themes that spoke of the passion EMS's consumers have for outdoor sports. They focused on the phrase break out, which refers to the feeling customers have when they "gotta get out" for a reinvigorating escape into the mountains. The team developed an icon that depicts a road leading up a high mountain toward a bright sun. The bold, sans serif oblique type treatment evokes action. The green and gold color palette spells out in no uncertain terms that EMS is about outdoor adventures.

EMS is about outdoor adventure, and its green and gold color palette supports that message.

The Result

As intended, the logo has won the hearts of EMS's loyal clients and new customers since its launch in 2003. Desgrippe Gobé's team also developed a secondary logo system for use on branded products, from apparel and accessories to backpacks and sports gear.

A secondary logo was developed for use on EMS's branded products, which range from apparel and accessories to backpacks and sports gear.

Client: **BioExplorations**
San Francisco, California, USA

Agency: **Project6 Design**
Berkeley, California

Appealing to both adults and school-age kids, the BioExplorations logo promises adventure in natural settings. The company conducts eco-camps and expeditions that allow travelers to interact with real-life scientists.

The Challenge

BioExplorations organizes and conducts eco-camps for school-age children, offering hands-on adventure programs to teach them about nature and science. The company also leads adult expeditions that combine travel, adventure, education, and science, giving participants a rare opportunity to interact with real-life scientists. Since BioExplorations's target market consists of both children and adults, the job of designing its logo challenged Project6 Design to develop an identity that would appeal to both audiences.

The Process

The Project6 Design team explored elements of nature to help steer the brand toward biology rather than biotechnology. Using a leaf as a part of the typography in the wordmark also aided in the visual breakup of a long name. The tagline supports the message that unites nature and travel, adding the stimulating words *adventure science* to the final equation. Professional and at the same time playful, the logo is accompanied by a palette of soft earth and water tones to continue the natural theme.

The Result

Response from parents, children, and teachers has been strong. In the initial stages, a website and a trifold flyer distributed to schools and parents were also developed for the client. Additional marketing, registration materials, and the company's stationery program followed.

A leaf incorporated into the logo reminds both young and old viewers that the adventure programs aren't just about science and discovery.

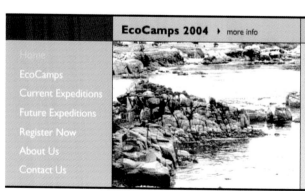

A palette of soft earth and water tones is used throughout BioExplorations' website, reinforcing the adventure programs' natural settings and appealing to both young and adult audiences.

Client: **SPIC—Spanish People in Control**
               Brooklyn, New York, USA

Agency: **The Missive**
               New York, New York

The Challenge

During the 1970s, ethnic pride was the realm of revolutionaries who sought change and employed T-shirts, headgear, and badges as vehicles for the symbols of their stated cause. The current trend toward customization and individuality in fashion and accessories has seen the reincorporation of powerful political statements into apparel and accessory designs reminiscent of the flags once worn by young political activists.

SPIC (Spanish People in Control) is a Brooklyn-based fashion and accessories retailer that wanted a strong ethnocentric statement on its summer 2004 product line. An acronym can, in itself, be a major design hurdle simply because it begs for a conventional solution. But the real challenge The Missive confronted was that the T-shirt and watch collection needed a bold graphic presence that could be legible in a variety of applications while representing the pride and diversity of this large—and growing—population.

The Process

For the sake of legibility, The Missive blended the acronym and its literal meaning into a clean typographic treatment, using Helvetica as its base. The brand's color palette takes its influence from the blues and yellows found in the national flags of many Latin countries, intended to represent all Latinos living in the United States.

The Result

Swatch has expressed strong interest in licensing the brand for its fashion watch collection. In addition, the identity's color palette has received broad approval from its target audience.

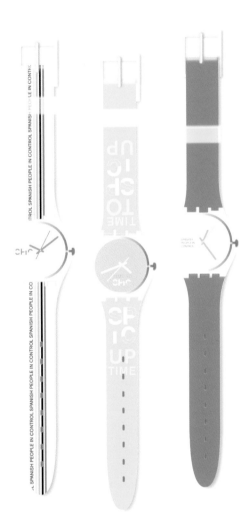

To bring instant comprehension to their client's acronym, The Missive encapsulated each word within its letter.

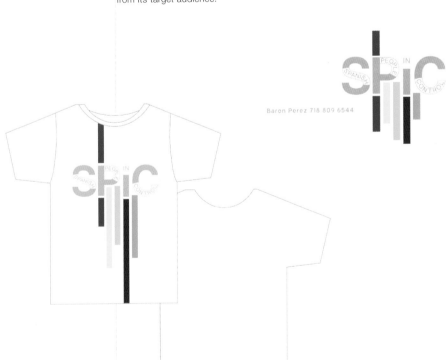

Baron Perez 718 809 6544

Mark McLaughlin
1682 Sunset Cliffs Boulevard
San Diego, California 92107 USA
619-546-9330
mark@mclaughlindesign.com
65, 66, 165

The Missive
305 West 20th Street
New York, New York 10011 USA
212-604-0421
gfx@nassor.com
25, 26, 27, 32, 69, 70, 118, 189

Modern Dog Design Company
7903 Greenwood Avenue NW
Seattle, Washington 98103 USA
206-789-7667
bubbles@moderndog.com
14, 15, 16, 179

Morpheus Studios
31 Hounslow Drive NW
Calgary, Alberta Canada
403-816-5143
greg@morpheus-studios.com
17

Murphy Design
1216 Arch Street, Suite 2C
Philadelphia, Pennsylvania 19107 USA
215-977-7093
rosemary@murphydesign.net
75, 86, 140, 141, 153

Outside the Box Interactive LLC
130 West 25th Street, Second Floor
New York, New York 10001 USA
212-463-7160
marketing@outboxin.com
81

Panagrafik
P.O. Box 8206
Bend, Oregon 97708 USA
541-382-3594
tparsons@panagrafik.com
99, 181

Project6 Design
2111 Fifth Street
Berkeley, California 94710 USA
510-540-8005
edina@project6.com
76, 168, 188

Richard Zeid Design
321 Custer Avenue #2E
Evanston, Illinois 60202 USA
847-864-0208
rzeid@rzdesign.com
18, 42, 158

Staple Design
156 Allen Street
New York, New York 10002 USA
212-979-8020
jeff@stapledesign.com
19, 105, 159, 180, 182

Staple Design
1-3-18 Chuo-Cho, Meguro
Tokyo 152-0001 Japan
19, 105, 159, 180, 182

Studio GT&P
Via Ariosto, 5
06034 Foligno (PG) Italy
39-0742-320372
info@tobanelli.it
83, 89, 120, 121, 134, 135

TAK Designs, LLC
P.O. Box 418
Baker City, Oregon 97814 USA
541-403-0330
info@takdesigns.com
155, 156

ThinkingCouch Interactive
71B Tras Street
Singapore 079010 Singapore
65-62246572
tiennee@thingcouch.com
137, 146, 162

Turner Duckworth
164 Townsend Street #8
San Francisco, California 94107 USA
415-495-8691
elize@turnerduckworth.com
55, 56–57, 58, 59, 100, 110, 113, 114,
115, 116, 128, 132

Turner Duckworth (UK)
Voysey House, Barley Mow Passage
London W4 4PH UK
44-8994-7190
44-8994-7192 (fax)
moira@turnerduckworth.co.uk
55, 56–57, 58, 59, 100, 110, 113, 114,
115, 116, 128, 132

UTOWA
17 West 18th Street
New York, New York 10011 USA
212-929-2400
info@utowa.com
164

Visible Theory
1005 East Colorado Boulevard, Suite 208
Pasadena, California 91101 USA
626-795-1885
scott@visibletheory.com
163

Walk Design
400 Cold Spring Road, Ph 18
Rocky Hill, Connecticut 06067 USA
860-983-4269
walkdesign@hotmail.com
20–21, 51

Wolff Olins
10 Regent's Wharf, All Saints Street
London N1 9RL UK
44-020-7713-7733
infolondon@wolff-olins.com
24, 64, 90–91, 144–145

Zurek Design
3581 Southwood Drive
Easton, Pennsylvania 18045 USA
610-253-0512
pamela@zurekdesign.com
154, 167

 **About the Authors**

Anistatia Miller is creative director for Bratskeir & Company, a New York–based marketing and corporate communications agency. She and **Jared Brown**, her coauthor and husband, are also contributing editors for *Gotham*, *Hamptons*, and *LA Confidential* magazines. Former contributing editors to *Adobe* magazine, Miller and Brown authored the Rockport books *What Logos Do and How They Do It* (1998), *Design Sense: Graphic Design on a Limited Budget* (1998), *Graphic Design Speak: A Visual Dictionary for Designers and Clients* (1999), and *Global Graphics: Symbols* (2001).

 **Acknowledgments**

Our heartfelt thanks to the many talented people who contributed their work and stories to this book. Our appreciation also goes out to Rockport's Kristin Ellison and Rochelle Bourgault, who kept us in line and on target throughout the project. Thank you all.